W9-BKP-146

Beyond the Bubble

2007
J. S.

Beyond
the Bubble

HOW TO KEEP THE REAL ESTATE MARKET
IN PERSPECTIVE—AND PROFIT
NO MATTER WHAT HAPPENS

Michael C. Thomsett
and Joshua Kahr

AMACOM

American Management Association

New York • Atlanta • Brussels • Chicago • Mexico City • San Francisco
Shanghai • Tokyo • Toronto • Washington, D.C.

Special discounts on bulk quantities of AMACOM books are available to corporations, professional associations, and other organizations. For details, contact Special Sales Department, AMACOM, a division of American Management Association, 1601 Broadway, New York, NY 10019.
Tel: 212-903-8316. Fax: 212-903-8083.
E-mail: specialsls@amanet.org
Website: www.amacombooks.org/go/specialsales
To view all AMACOM titles go to: www.amacombooks.org

This publication is designed to provide accurate and authoritative information in regard to the subject matter covered. It is sold with the understanding that the publisher is not engaged in rendering legal, accounting, or other professional service. If legal advice or other expert assistance is required, the services of a competent professional person should be sought.

REALTOR® is a registered collective membership mark that identifies a real estate professional who is a member of the National Association of REALTORS® and subscribes to its strict Code of Ethics. AMACOM uses these names throughout this book in initial capital letters or ALL CAPITAL letters for editorial purposes only, with no intention of trademark violation.

Library of Congress Cataloging-in-Publication Data

Thomsett, Michael C.
    Beyond the bubble : how to keep the real estate market in perspective—and profit no matter what happens / Michael C. Thomsett and Joshua Kahr.
        p. cm.
    Includes bibliographical references and index.
    ISBN-10: 0-8144-7409-8
    ISBN-13: 978-0-8144-7409-9
    1. Real estate investment—United States.   2. Speculation—United States.   3. Financial crises—United States.   4. Real property—Valuation—United States.   I. Kahr, Joshua   II. Title.

HD255.T495   2007
333.33'220973—dc22   2006029431

© 2007 Michael C. Thomsett and Joshua Kahr.
All rights reserved.
Printed in the United States of America.

This publication may not be reproduced,
stored in a retrieval system,
or transmitted in whole or in part,
in any form or by any means, electronic,
mechanical, photocopying, recording, or otherwise,
without the prior written permission of AMACOM,
a division of American Management Association,
1601 Broadway, New York, NY 10019.

Printing number

10   9   8   7   6   5   4   3   2   1

Contents

Acknowledgments

Our thanks to the entire editorial staff at AMACOM for their consistent professionalism and help throughout this project. We also thank our research assistant Ilan Grunwald, who found valuable information and pulled it together from many sources.

—Michael C. Thomsett and Joshua Kahr

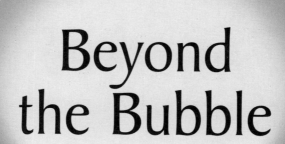

The Nature of
Real Estate Bubbles

In 1973, I purchased my first home in Marin County (just north of San Francisco) for $29,400. My father was appalled at seeing me spend so much for property. He predicted that I would never make a profit. But sixteen years later, in 1989, I sold the home for $325,000. Virtually all of the increase in value happened in the local bubble between 1987 and 1989.

What caused this dramatic surge in housing prices in Marin County over such a short period of time? There were a couple of key factors at work. First, long-term drought conditions caused Marin County to impose a water moratorium for several years, which prevented virtually *all* residential-home building. When the moratorium was lifted in 1987, prices for existing houses skyrocketed. Second, many large employers left San Francisco proper and relocated in the surrounding areas after the city passed a payroll tax. Fireman's Fund alone brought tens of thousands of jobs to Marin County in a single year, placing even more demand on local housing stock.

The Marin County bubble could have been predicted if you knew what to look for: a mostly fixed number of houses in the area, the likelihood that water restrictions eventually would be lifted, and the sudden influx of a large number of potential home buyers. This is a typical example of the kinds of factors that cause real estate bubbles. The person quoted above didn't see any appreciable increase in the value of his house for almost fourteen years. But consider someone who bought a house for, say, $35,000 in 1985 and sold it four years later for over $300,000!

Bubbles can be extremely profitable or very dangerous. Prices rise and prices fall, inevitably, so bubbles cannot continue forever. This book examines the bubble phenomenon in real estate and the rest of the economy. It explains what factors create bubbles, shows how you can predict them if you know what to look for, and provides suggestions for dealing with potential sudden changes in valuation.

THE BIG PICTURE

Beyond the Bubble explains and examines the real estate bubble in a context of a larger investment market and the overall economy. This is important because it helps to understand how and why bubbles emerge and, historically, what has happened to earlier bubbles. Once you study the broader markets and bubbles in this context, you will be able to develop an awareness of key market drivers affecting real estate prices, both economic and noneconomic. As a result, you will be better able to evaluate markets and predict the rise and fall of prices.

The book also examines real estate by specific type, because it is important for you to view residential and other types of real estate as entirely different markets. Just as regional factors dictate how bubbles act, the different kinds of real estate perform based on vastly dissimilar economic and market forces.

REGIONAL FACTORS

When there appears to be a nationwide real estate bubble, there is a widespread belief or assumption that when the bubble bursts, it will do so universally. This is highly unlikely. Real estate valuation tends to respond to regional and local influences; there is no single real estate market.

Clearly, there are vast differences between the markets in Los Angeles, Phoenix, St. Petersburg, Sioux Falls, and New York City. All of these markets have specific characteristics, but they are different in each place. The levels of jobs, commuter trends, college-aged population and retirees, local economic forces (industry versus farming, for example) and dozens of other factors define those regional markets. You have to know what's going on in your market and with the type of property you're investing in.

Some books propose drastic measures in preparation for the "coming crash" in real estate. But this presupposes that your house is going to lose value no matter where you live. The alarmist approach to real estate is not as realistic or as sensible as studying the factors in *your* region and then deciding whether or not you are exposed to an actual bubble. Generalized advice on how to protect yourself before the bubble bursts is not relevant if, in fact, you have low exposure to a real estate bubble. If you do have high exposure, you may want to take drastic action; but the first step should be to study your local market.

When the bubble does burst in any one region, it will occur for very exact reasons relating to the local market. Those cause-and-effect situations are not universal, so the Sioux Falls market will not react in the same way as the markets of New York, Florida, or Arizona. There is no such thing as a single bubble, and even in the regions where prices have risen and bubbles have emerged, the future changes in value will not occur at the same time or for the same reasons. The Marin County bubble burst in 1989 when the earthquake hit; property values fell over the next six months. However, after this slump, housing prices rebounded with a vengeance. And as of 2006, a longer-term bubble in the area made San Francisco one of the fastest-growing regions in the country.

ROOT CAUSES

A bubble in real estate or any other commodity does not occur without reason. This book examines the root causes of bubbles, and how those causes are likely to change in the future. For example, one cause for rapid rise in residential prices in many areas is the trend in interest rates. As rates move lower, larger segments of the population are able to qualify for financing. As a result, there is increased demand for housing, which drives up prices. Eventually, as interest rates rise, those prices are likely to stop growing and remain flat, or even to fall.

Another root cause involves the location of housing and the people who want to move to those locations. The greater Phoenix and central Florida areas have become favorite retirement centers, and as a result a lot of construction has occurred.

But there are consequences. For example, Phoenix used to be known for its clean air and safe living conditions. Today, it is one of the most smog-polluted cities in the country, which may surprise people who remember past reasons for migration to Arizona.[1] It is the size of that migration and the related increase in the use of autos that have, in fact, changed the situation. The attraction of an area can lead to its loss of that very attraction. Phoenix has also experienced increases in crime rates and is now among one of the most dangerous places to live.[2] Changes have occurred in other cities as well. For example, in Las Vegas, *the* hot property market only a few years ago, property values have recently declined more than 20 percent.

* * *

These are some of the many factors affecting the duration and movement of bubbles. As population trends cause rapid development, increases in crime and pollution follow. When you combine the effects of traditional economic factors (those falling within the realm of supply and demand) with the more esoteric noneconomic factors (so-called quality-of-life factors like climate, crime levels, and traffic), you encompass the *range* of possible influences of real estate prices. When any of the overall factors start to arise, a bubble is likely to occur over some period of time. When more than two of these influences are at work, bubbles can be dramatic, rapid, and large. For speculators, these opportunities are appealing. But the more speculators enter the market, the more their impact will be on the bubble itself. Just as pollution and crime levels affect the real estate bubble, so does the level of speculation. It is among the factors adding to and even aggravating the bubble itself.

These days, real estate bubbles have become the norm rather than the exception. Everyone who owns property or is considering buying has to ask the same questions: When is a good time to buy? Should I sell to avoid loss? How do I recognize the signs? *Beyond the Bubble* is intended as a study of these questions and a source for answers.

NOTES

1. American Lung Association, "The Most Polluted Cities," 2004, reported on www.citymayors.com.
2. The Phoenix-Mesa-Scottsdale metro area was ranked the 23rd most dangerous place out of 369 cities studied, based on a 2005 survey by Morgan Quitno (12th Annual, "City Crime Rankings"): www.morganquitno.com.

Real Estate and the Rest of the Economy

O nly a few decades ago, the United States (and most of the rest of the world) operated on the "gold standard." Essentially, this meant that currency in circulation was backed up by gold reserves. This had the effect of keeping the economy in check, limiting growth, and preventing many economic bubbles, including those in real estate.

Under the gold standard, prices could only move up or down to a degree, and they could not run out of control or in excess of the real demand for real estate. Today, forces other than traditional "supply and demand" control the market, enabling prices to rise at incredible rates, and to bubble. The bubbles we see today—where inflated prices exist and are expected at some point to burst—are a consequence of widespread speculation in real estate. Property flipping, overdevelopment, and leveraged real estate investing all contribute to this. In addition, many areas have experienced real estate bubbles due to demographic factors, such as population migration and baby boomer retirement.

2007

No market operates in isolation. Real estate values do not move upward or downward just because people want to own their own homes. That is a factor, of course; but there are many more factors at play. Often, these factors creating or affecting valuation lead to bubbles, distorting the value of real estate.

In order to understand real estate in general and real estate bubbles in particular, you must make a distinction between "valuation" and current "market value." These two are not necessarily the same, although the terms are often mixed up. Most people tend to think that there is no difference.

Valuation is an assessed or appraised price for real estate based on logical comparisons and costs. Thus, the cost of materials and land, comparisons between properties in similar neighborhoods, and other logical criteria are used to establish the valuation of property. In a real estate bubble, valuation may be distorted by artificial demand and other causes, leading to rapid increases in market value, which, eventually, has to be corrected.

Market value is simply the price that a buyer and seller agree to. In an orderly market, a property's market value will be based on appraisal and valuation principles. But in a real estate bubble, the principles of valuation may be suspended or ignored entirely.

HOW SPECULATION FEVER FEEDS BUBBLES

To grasp how bubbles work, it is useful to examine how speculators think, and how illogic can drive prices unreasonably high. Many books try to blame real estate bubbles on excessive credit, low interest rates, or liberal lending policies. Although all of these factors influence the bubbles, they are by no means a sole cause. Bubbles have always popped up in history, regardless of monetary policy, international trade, or other direct causes. It seems that speculators always find a way.

Analysis of economic trends can explain a lot. The U.S. trade imbalance, federal deficit, and monetary policy all contribute to the bubble. But these do not explain the periodic recurrence of bubbles and they are not as instructive as a study of human nature. Even with the economic factors in play, the simple fact is that in all sorts of economic times, *greed* drives economic bubbles. When investors and speculators see prices rising, they want to get into the market and get a piece of the action. The more speculators, the greater the artificial demand; the bubble feeds itself until it cannot grow any longer, and then it bursts.

Pyramid Schemes

Take a look at the most basic form of bubble, the pyramid scheme. The typical scheme pops up now and then in offices and plants, among friends and social contacts, or on the Internet. These schemes are illegal, but their appeal is the apparent simplicity and ease with which people are promised great riches. In fact, only the originators (and perhaps a few friends) make money, while most (usually 85 percent or more) lose all of their money.

The basic idea for the pyramid scheme is that people pay money in over a series of levels, and at each level the number of people grows. If a pyramid begins with one person collecting one dollar from six other people, he makes a $6 profit. If those six each go to six other people (total of 36), the level and the number grow. So in theory, by the time the pyramid reaches 13 levels, everyone gets rich:

Level	People
1	6
2	36
3	216
4	1,296
5	7,776
6	46,656
7	279,936
8	1,679,616
9	10,077,696
10	60,466,176
11	362,797,056
12	2,176,782.336
13	13,060,694,016

The pyramid scheme argument goes as follows: If each person at each level gets six other people to each pay in one dollar, everyone can get very rich. At the end of 11 levels, over 362 million people are involved, and at one dollar each, that is a fantastic amount of money. Of course, this number is greater than the population of the United States; and the 13 billion people at level 13 are more than the population of the entire world.

It should be abundantly clear to you that pyramid schemes are just that—schemes. They are plans by which a relatively large number of people are compelled to transfer money to a relatively small number of people. As illogical as this concept is, and as clearly as it can be shown that it doesn't work, people fall victim to pyramid schemes every day. Today, with the convenience of the Internet, the opportunities for online bubble scams are greater than ever. Even a decade ago, the Federal Trade Commission (FTC) concluded that chain letters are among the most common scams passed around by e-mail.[1]

Appeals to Greed

By definition, a pyramid scheme is the exchange of money without any underlying tangible value. As such, it is illogical and a model of an economic bubble. It is impossible for wealth to be created out of nothing, yet this is the false logic driving most bubbles. Only those few people at the very beginning of the chain make money; most lose.

Chain letters and similar pyramid schemes are correctly lumped in with other types of speculation fever. They are appeals to greed and they find willing takers easily because of that. If you apply these ideas to the *preconstruction* condo market (speculators purchasing condos before they are built and then selling them before completion) that is running rampant in Miami-Dade County, Florida, the same type of bubble is built up. Speculators see recent examples of people doubling their money in less than a month, and they want to get in on the deal. They don't stop to look at the growing rate of construction, which approaches a decade's worth of demand; nor do they stop to question where the run-up in prices will end. Because profits have been made recently, speculators refuse to ask questions, downplay the dangers, and invest all they can. So the bubble grows and grows.

Just as money cannot be created and expanded indefinitely through a chain letter, real estate values cannot continue upward without end. A bubble will eventually burst. But just as speculation fever involving a chain letter will eventually disintegrate, that does not mean that everyone will be affected by a bubble. For example, in a four-story office building, a company on the second floor may have a chain letter being passed around and dozens of people are likely to lose money. But the people on the first, third, and fourth floors—where the chain letter does not go—are not going to suffer any consequences.

The same distinction has to be made in real estate bubbles.

Abuses and speculation in Florida will not affect the market anywhere else in the country. In fact, if the problem is limited to the Miami area, there is no reason to expect the rest of the state to also experience a burst bubble—unless the abuses in the preconstruction market has spread to other areas. There is evidence, in fact, that similar speculation has spread to Fort Lauderdale and other southern Florida cities, which means that when the condo market bubble does burst it probably will affect all of those communities at about the same time. But any community where speculative activity in preconstruction condos is not underway will not be affected directly. Some residual affect is to be expected from the economic ripple effect that will result any time a bubble bursts; but as a general rule, real estate values outside of an area are not going to be devastated. The factors determining valuation of real estate are always local, and the consequences of bursting bubbles are always localized.

DEMAND LEVELS AND STRENGTH OF THE MARKET

You now can understand bubbles by comparing real estate to pyramid schemes; in fact, the same math flaw applies. Eventually, the market for further speculation is exhausted and inflated values tumble. So the distinction between valuation (what property is worth based on actual market forces) and current market value (what buyers are willing to pay) *should* be minimal and usually is. When a bubble has formed, the gap between these two widens until a sudden adjustment occurs.

There are three methods for judging the general conditions of demand and strength of the market (in other words, to decide whether buyers or sellers are in charge), and what the current trend reveals about the direction of change within the market. These three—inventory on the market, spread, and time on the market—are a wise starting point in evaluating conditions in your city or town.

Inventory on the Market

You can discover one of the more glaring symptoms that your local real estate market is in a bubble when you check the inventory of homes for sale on the market. Ideally, the current level should be a good match for demand within the coming six to twelve months. So if, in a typical month, 200 homes sell in your city, an inventory of 1,200 to 2,400 homes is reasonable. Sellers want as small an inventory as possible because that reduces the supply and keeps prices high. Buyers prefer a larger inventory because it provides more to choose from, including bargains.

A bubble can be defined on the basis of inventory as well. In Miami-Dade County, Florida, at the beginning of 2006, there were enough condo units being built to satisfy a nine-year supply. That fact should make it clear to everyone that, at some point, the bubble has to burst. There is simply no support in the market for that level of construction and activity, which was driven almost entirely by speculation.

In your region, you may study inventory as part of a trend, and that information is readily available through local brokerage firms or lenders. Today's number is valuable, but it only takes on significance when you see the direction of the trend. All analysis of the local market has to include properties under construction and planned, because within a year or two those properties will be on the market. So when you study local inventory, you get the best information by analyzing where the inventory has been each month during the past year, in which direction it is moving, and how quickly the situation is changing.

The Spread

The difference between asked price and sales price also reveals the health of your real estate market. As a general rule, in a healthy economy, the spread will be less than 5 percent. But even this is a generalization, because every region is unique and cannot be treated to a blanket "rule of thumb" about numbers. But using 5 percent as a yardstick, you would expect to see properties listed at $200,000 to be sold for an average of $190,000 or more. So what happens when final sales prices begin to slip lower than this, meaning the spread is getting larger? It means the market is getting softer, and that buyers are not willing to pay as much now as they were last month, two months ago, or six months ago.

In a real estate bubble, you see the opposite effect, at least while the bubble is expanding. Real estate bubbles tend to be accompanied by a "buying frenzy," which includes illogical actions and reactions. Buyers offer far more than properties are worth, driving prices higher and higher, and causing appraisers to shake their heads in disbelief; and yet, the trend continues. You can recognize the height of a bubble when—often for a very brief time span—offers are made on properties *above* the asked price. When people are willing to pay a higher price than the seller has asked, the market is exceptionally hot.

A problem with analyzing the spread is that it consists of averages. So if your city is experiencing a spread averaging only 3 percent, what does that mean? It could mean that there are numerous properties selling at 5 percent below the asked price, while many others are selling at some level *above* the asked price. A bubble also can exist in a narrow slice of the market (such as in the condo market, beachfront properties, or specific neighborhoods). So as valuable as it is to look at the trend represented by the spread, you also need to break down the numbers to identify the entire picture of what is going on.

Time on the Market

The third test of your local market is the time it takes from the listing of properties to the sold date. The standard observation is that in hot markets, time on the market shrinks to a relatively small number; and in very cold markets, time expands to several months. So these "seller's markets" and "buyer's markets" are convenient labels that accurately describe the overall conditions in one region, but they do not always give you the whole story. Any time you are dealing in averages, the real trend can be easily obscured.

Just as the spread changes in a bubble and, from a real estate agent's perspective, actually improves, time on the market can seem positive, especially as bubbles grow. Any real estate professional is likely to tell you that when the time shrinks, it is a positive sign. However, this is exactly what happens in the buying frenzy of the real estate bubble. As prices rise, fueled by speculation, more and more people come into the picture. Logically, the time on the market will shrink as today's speculators turn over properties at faster and faster rates. Generally, a fast turnaround in real estate is "healthy" for the real estate economy, but you need to know the components of time on the market to determine whether the turnaround is being driven by actual demand, or by the artificial demand of a bubble.

Here again, averages obscure the real trend. You need to examine the classes or properties to decide what is happening. As a general rule, more expensive properties take longer to sell, and cheaper properties turn over more quickly. So when you find that over the past year, time on the market has gone from 78 days down to 42 days, it would appear to be an extremely positive trend. It implies that demand is growing and properties are selling at a faster clip. But upon examining the components, you might discover that two separate trends are underway. For example, higher-priced homes may be selling at the same rate as one year ago, while newly constructed, far cheaper homes are turning over at accelerated rates. Interpreting the significance of these offsetting trends is a matter of also reviewing price changes over time. However, the point here is that the average is not the whole story of real estate valuation and trends. To find out what is really occurring in the market, a more in-depth analysis is required.

THE TEN PRINCIPLES OF VALUATION

The most common method for judging real estate is price. This factor is easily found, since it is the primary information provided by sellers and real estate agents. In fact, people most often search by price, and only after finding the range they want do they ask other questions about the size, features, condition, and location of the property.

So great is the emphasis on price that it may distract you from looking at other features affecting valuation. Price is the most apparent feature of bubbles because, as prices climb higher and higher, more people want to be a part of the frenzy. But once you appreciate the ten principles of valuation, you realize that price is not the whole story. In fact, these ten principles help to explain real estate bubbles:

1. Anticipation

This principle states that "current market value is affected by expectations about *future* value." This is seen in the stock market, where the price/earnings ratio summarizes a stock's price as a multiple of future earnings.

The same type of anticipation is experienced in the real estate market. If people believe that values are going to go up, that belief fuels increasing prices. Thus, real estate bubbles become strong and remain so because of anticipation. They are self-fulfilling in this regard. Local plans for land—such as rezoning, new construction, dedicated parklands, and rerouted highways—also affect perceptions about future value.

2. Change

The belief that "change is a constant and changes in real estate are inevitable" is witnessed in many ways. As population size and mix changes, as jobs rise and fall, and dozens of other local factors emerge, real estate values follow suit.

It is quite easy for observers to see rising prices as reflecting actual change in the market when, in fact, the demand is artificial. So rising prices are not caused by the old standard beliefs concerning supply and demand; they are not occurring because of real or long-term change. It is thus important to make a distinction between permanent change and shorter-term, bubble-driven effects.

3. Competition

This concept states that "whenever the potential exists for profit, competition will result." So when property values begin to rise in a region, it tends to attract buyers, who want to invest profitably. This observation applies to homeowners, investors, and speculators alike. In any system where the market sets value, competition will also exist.

This may also create or contribute to real estate bubbles. Because everyone wants to profit from their investments, speculators may actually create greater demand through their competitive efforts. But this "essence of the bubble" itself will ultimately lead to a collapse, because it cannot be sustained. Just as any pyramid scheme collapses after only a few plateaus, when real estate prices are not based on *real* competition in the marketplace, they will eventually have to correct, which means that prices will fall.

4. Conformity

Conformity is the principle that states, "Real estate will be the most profitable when it is the same as or similar to other properties in the same area." This principle surprises many people because it is not obvious. Unfortunately, some discover its impact only after they have purchased a nonconforming property. So if the typical house on a street is on a standard 50×100-foot lot, contains three bedrooms and two baths, and is 1,800 square feet, that becomes the norm. If *your* house is on a double lot, has five bedrooms and three baths, and is 3,500 square feet, it is nonconforming. When property values rise in the area, the non-conforming house will not rise at the same rate as the conforming properties.

Bubbles tend to occur in very concentrated regions and in very typical properties. So if the bubble involves the preconstruction condo market, it does not necessarily affect all properties, or even all condo units. If the bubble-sensitive properties sell in the range of $150,000 to $650,000, it is likely that a $2 million, beachfront condo will not be affected. The principle of conformity can be used to help define the extent of bubble risk (the potential for loss if and when the bubble bursts) by observing what types of properties are experiencing rapid price increases. Invariably you will discover that a very specific type of property is being affected and is at risk, and that other properties not matching the conforming criteria are not going to be affected at all or to the same extent when the bubble bursts.

5. Contribution

An important distinction has to be made between the cost of an improvement, and how much that improvement adds to value. Contribution expresses the fact that "improvement costs are not always equal to the dollar amount that the contribution adds to market value." For example, many people have discovered that putting in a swimming pool adds little or no market value (in some cases, it may even reduce market value). On the other hand, a relatively inexpensive exterior paint job may add much more to market value than it actually costs. Contribution may vary in either direction.

The problem with real estate bubbles is that market values continue rising, often at levels exaggerated far above market-driven equity. In other words, there exists no real contribution to market value. Thus, even when bubbles are driven by actual demand, contribution lags behind. For example, bubble-driven prices have risen in many areas when interest rates were falling between 2001 and 2005. More and more people qualified for financing and bought new homes. This growth in demand was very real, but what happens when interest rates begin to rise? If variable-rate mortgage rates start climbing, many families who qualified marginally for those new homes may no longer be able to afford payments. In this example, the contribution—consisting of greater demand for homes—created higher market value, but that market value itself was vulnerable to interest rates. The general tendency is to view market value as strictly driven by supply and demand. In this case, however, interest rates had a more significant impact.

6. Highest and Best Use

This principle dictates that "value will be the greatest when property is utilized in the best way." Thus, orderly zoning and land-use laws serve a distinct purpose in helping to ensure that land use makes sense in any specific location. No one wants a quarry located in the middle of a residential neighborhood, for example. Property is suitably located for specific uses, including residential, commercial, industrial, and agricultural uses. Uniformity enables city planning to map out land uses so that the highest and best use of land is possible.

Suitability is, in fact, central to this concept; but when real estate bubbles occur, they don't necessarily affect the highest and best use of property. If a residential neighborhood consists mainly of owner-occupied housing, and this is part of the zoning mandate for the area, nothing has changed except the market value (which may be driven by low interest rates, population and employment changes, or other direct causes). But when property values are driven upward due to speculation, that is not the highest and best use of land. Returning to the example of Miami-Dade, the construction of condo units has been driven the last few years by seemingly unending supplies of speculators. There are not enough people in the area to buy and live in those units, so the construction itself is driven by the speculative bubble. In this situation, the bubble eventually bursts and values fall.

7. Plottage

This is a somewhat obscure valuation principle, but an important one. The rule observes that "value tends to be greatest when land in a single area is combined and put to use for a single purpose." For example, in one area a number of varying parcels of land are owned by individuals. A developer buys up all of the land and acquires a total of seven acres, and then develops that land to create a new residential subdivision. This would only be possible through the acquisition under single ownership, because dozens of individual owners would not have the ability or the capital to work together to develop the land.

This principle is distorted when speculators acquire land specifically to increase its value, with the idea of turning around and reselling for a profit. Everyone has heard the story about a "land grab" in which an evil developer turns a huge profit by buying up plots from unsuspecting elderly widows. This stereotype is not as common as some people believe, but land speculation does create a bubble. However, if the bubble is created as part of a larger development plan, it is possible that the speculation will pay off.

Not all bubbles end up bursting. Some create profits for the speculators and may even benefit the community. For example, when the Disney company bought land in the Orlando area, it certainly had the effect of increasing land values. But the development of Disney World and all of the surrounding attractions generates a lot of tax revenue and brings millions of tourists to the area. That would not be possible without the order and consistency of plottage. The bubble created through the consolidation of land did not lead to a decline in value, but increased it.

8. Progression

Under this principle, "real estate values tend to increase when other, similar properties of greater quality are constructed in the same area." So if a home is worth $225,000, and other homes in the same area are built and sold for an average of $250,000, the principle of progression tells you that the lower-priced home is likely to increase in value to approach or meet the average price. The adage, "buy the worst house on a good block" is one expression of the principle of progression.

Some residential real estate bubbles reflect the concept of progression on a broad scale. For example, if a city has older stock of homes but those are being gradually replaced, renovated, and upgraded to modern standards, progression may create a bubble in the prices of *all* property. Given the assumption that values are appreciating and are not inhibited due to soft demand, the tendency is for older, outdated homes to appreciate at a greater rate than newer homes of the same size and with the same features.

9. Regression

This is the opposite of progression. This principle states that "real estate values tend to fall when other, similar properties of *lower* quality are constructed in the same area." For example, if you buy a nice home in an area where other homes are being built of lower quality, your property value is not likely to rise; instead it is likely to fall to approach the norm for the area.

There is a tendency to make two general assumptions about property values. First is that value is individual, that each property's market value depends on its features without regard to other properties in the same area. The second is the idea that putting more money into a property increases its market value, even if other homes in the area are not being improved or updated.

Both of these ideas are misguided. The principle of regression makes the point that the surrounding trends have more to do with market value than the amount of money invested in one property. You cannot depend on a single-property bubble created by updating the kitchen, painting the exterior, and spending money on landscaping. If other homes in the area are run-down, you won't be able to get a return on your investment, which is why you have to pick properties with a broader view.

10. Substitution

Under the principle of substitution, "real estate values are going to be limited by the value of other properties of the same type." Appraisers seek comparable properties (comps) as a starting point in setting value for residential property. Comps are made up of recent sales of homes in the same or similar neighborhoods, with the same features, condition, and size as the subject property. Because exact substitutions are not always located, appraisers make adjustments in the appraised value to allow for variations in size, condition, features, age, and other mitigating factors. The principle of substitution is closely associated with the principles of conformity, progression, and regression.

The disturbing fact about real estate bubbles is that they often cause growth in market value without any regard for the principle of substitution. Values simply continue to rise. Speculators and homeowners alike may see the market value of their homes double in a three-year period, even though appraisers cannot explain how or why this occurs. The bubble is invariably a distortion of what is usually an orderly and logical application of the market, and substitution makes this point when a specific property is compared to recent sales. How can you compare today's property to a sale three months ago if values have in the meantime gone up 20 percent? Prices in real estate are as chaotic in the short term as in other markets. The trick is to determine whether those prices are persistent over time.

*   *   *

Real estate principles explain how value *should* be set. But valuation and market value are by no means identical. Valuation is an estimate of what a property's sales price should be based on an application of the ten principles of valuation. Market value is the number a seller can get from a buyer. So in a real estate bubble, the market value of property may rise in complete contradiction to these principles. The *perception of value* is far more important in where that number falls than any actual, logic-based valuation principle.

THE THREE TYPES OF REAL ESTATE MARKETS

A lot of buyers are aware of the basic economic model for supply and demand. More demand pushes up prices, and too much supply pushes them down. But in attempting to understand how bubbles work, you need to be aware that there are three separate and distinct "markets" at work at the same time. The best-known is the supply/demand market. But you also need to be aware of the rental market and the financing market. Each of the three markets affects prices in different ways, but observing them together helps to explain how bubbles develop and how they evolve.

The Supply-and-Demand Market

This is thought of by most people as "the market" for real estate. Emphasis is placed on prices of properties, and changes in average price over time. The causes for price change are not widely understood, not even by experts. Clearly, *real demand* has a lot to do with prices moving higher in an area. Real demand is the need and desire for housing on the part of buyers, who intend to occupy those homes.

To coin a term for the purpose of making a distinction, the alternative kind of demand can be called *market-responsive demand*. This includes the realm of investors who purchase property to use as rentals, to fix up and resell, to buy at discount and flip, or to speculate within a rapidly moving bubble. These forms of demand are all quite real, so they are not the opposite of real demand, just a type of demand driven by different incentives. In extreme bubbles—for example, when speculators are causing excess construction in the belief that double-digit profits will be endless—the demand is purely bubble-driven and may be called *surreal demand*. No logical study of markets in the grasp of speculative fever can explain what drives the market higher and higher, and so "surreal" is an apt description. The good news is that bubble-driven markets tend to be isolated in terms of property type and location, so there will not be a nationwide burst in the real estate bubble due to surreal demand.

The supply side of this equation is equally interesting. *Real supply* will consist of newly constructed properties, or vacated existing properties that approximately match the demand. If 400 properties sell per year in your city, construction of 400 new properties per year (less existing properties that turn over) is a *real supply*. A *market-responsive* supply is created when market-responsive demand appears. Thus, developers may construct

new units because speculators are lining up to buy in preconstruction phases, even if no real demand is going to be there to
meet that supply.

The Rental Market

You can learn a lot about the condition of a region by studying
rental vacancy rates. When rates are quite low, strong demand
for rentals is apparent. This may be seasonal. For example, in
cities and towns with a large college population, month-to-month
rental demand might be quite high when school is in session,
and relatively weak in the summer months when students return
home. But a distinction has to be made between supply and demand for properties, and the rental market.

A strong rental market often goes hand in hand with demand
for owner-occupied properties. But it is also possible that variations in these two markets can coexist. So a city with little or no
employment opportunities and a population consisting of retirees and college students may experience low demand for new
homes and high demand for rentals. With few jobs available, the
population will not be increasing. And while college students
drive the rental market, they buy virtually no homes.

Real estate investors may assume that low vacancies are a
symptom of a strong real estate market, and they may purchase
single-family homes and rent them out. They may be able to generate cash flow to cover their mortgage, with the underlying assumption that the strong rental market also influences real estate
values. But while the property is owned, what does it mean when
market values remain flat? It's likely that property taxes will continue rising each year as the local county looks for new revenues;
but property values remain unchanged. A combined retirement
and college population is not going to do anything to drive the
market. Employment is flat and a large pool of college students
provides cheap labor for the many shops and service outlets in
local stores. But this situation provides no new market demand.

The Financing Market

The third market in real estate has a lot to do with the creation of bubbles. The financing market is expressed in most cases in terms of average mortgage interest rates. When rates fell between 2001 and 2005 to historically low levels, the population of people who could qualify for first-time mortgages expanded rapidly. This placed new *real demand* for housing on the market, and created a bubble. But when interest rates begin to rise, variable-rate mortgage payments rise as well, which slows down the bubble and increases the rate of housing defaults.

The potential problems homeowners face with rising interest rates should not be ignored. In recent years, low rates inspired a massive increase in the rate of loans issued and in financing terms as well. For example, in San Diego, California, 50 percent of all loans issued between 2003 and 2005 were either interest-only or variable-rate mortgages. Sharp increases in interest rates will affect everyone with these kinds of loans.[2]

Ironically, the financing market does not appear to directly affect real estate bubbles. A popular (but inaccurate) theory states that when interest rates rise, the bubble will burst. But look at the statistics for only one year, from 2004 to 2005: In Riverside County, California, lender default notices increased 43 percent in that year. But at the same time, median housing values in that same county rose 15.8 percent, from $354,000 up to $410,000.[3]

Delinquency rates continue to rise each year, not only in southern California but across many regions. Of residential properties in the U.S. in all areas (single-family homes and up to four-unit properties), involving a total of over 41 million loans, 4.7 percent were delinquent by the end of 2005, and each quarter's results inch higher.[4]

Some market observers shrug off the disparity between rising foreclosure rates and interest rate hikes. The argument goes that "in most of the country, anyone who has owned a home for even a year or two is likely sitting on enough equity to sell or refinance if the loan payments become unaffordable."[5] But this advice ignores the possibility of what will happen if the bubble does indeed burst in those very cities or towns where the price run-up was caused by rapid expansion of the demand markets. Foreclosures are one factor that can adversely affect housing values. So "enough" equity may exist on paper today, but that does not mean it will be there if there is a big correction in values.

EXTERNAL INFLUENCES ON REAL ESTATE

There may be any number of external influences that affect value beyond the three markets (supply/demand, rental, and financing). Bubbles form for a variety of reasons, not just increased real demand (or decreased real supply) or speculative activity. For example, natural disasters and environmental problems can have a significant effect on value.

Consider that after a particularly devastating hurricane season, lumber costs rise significantly, adding to construction prices, not just in the immediately affected areas, but everywhere. Or large numbers of people relocating due to major environmental problems can place upward price pressure on real estate in the areas to which the displaced people are moving.

Even without environmental or natural disasters affecting real estate values, increases in the costs of building materials can dramatically alter the housing picture. If import duties rise suddenly, it affects the cost of lumber across borders. The consequences of higher costs invariably lead to shifts in employment and population. In some cases, an increase in the cost of an item not directly related to housing also can have an effect. Steadily increasing gas prices, for example, can cause people to move closer to where they work.

Anyone who owns property or who is thinking about buying a home needs to be aware of how real estate works within the overall economy. But it is also important to zero in on what is happening in your own area. Chapter 2 examines the regional nature of real estate.

NOTES

1. FTC Names Its Dirty Dozen: 12 Scams Most Likely to Arrive via Bulk Email," July 1998, www.ftc.gov.
2. Real estate markets cool nationwide," *Inman News*, March 27, 2006.
3. Corey Washington, "Foreclosures Rise as Buyers Pay for Spree," *The Business Press*, March 13, 2006.
4. "Residential Mortgage Delinquencies Increase," press release, Mortgage Banker's Association, March 16, 2006.
5. Cybele Weisser, "Foreclosures: Bargain Hunters Beware!" *Money Magazine*, February 16, 2006.

CHAPTER 2

The Regional Character of Real Estate

N ews reports remind you, almost daily, that the real estate market is changing. Mortgage rates are at an all-time low, housing prices are going through the roof, and sales are booming. Then things change. Housing starts are down, mortgage rates are up, and sales are slowing down. But what does it all really mean?

National stories about real estate are always based on averages. But the real estate market in your city or town is regional and all of the changes in that market are going to be in reaction to what happens in your area. Watching averages is dangerous because it tells you nothing about what *you* can expect in your own investments. It is like picking stocks based on the Dow Jones Industrial Averages. Although that index does give you some hint about the general health and mood of the market, it does not tell you what is going to happen to any one stock.

Real estate is strictly regional, a feature not seen in other investments. Local and regional factors have far more to do with prices and value than any national averages. In fact, even national trends (unemployment, for example) do not really relate to prices of property locally. While the national averages include large-scale layoffs in Detroit, New York, and California, employment in your city may be booming; so what value are those averages?

When you consider the possibility of bubbles bursting and prices falling, you need to look at a combination of local and national trends. The only national trend that is likely to affect local property values directly is that of monetary policy. If rates rise, the continuation of a property bubble is going to be unlikely. Price growth will slow down and may even stop. In some cases, prices will fall. But if you have already bought property and if you have financed the purchase with a fixed-rate mortgage, those trends will not affect you.

Local influences on property valuation will include trends in population and the related changes in demand for housing; employment; and quality-of-life issues (crime statistics, traffic levels, and climate, for example).

COMPARING REGIONAL EXAMPLES

If you compare several different regions in terms of real estate valuation, you'll immediately see how local influences greatly affect property value. You'll also see that these things are not universal—so it's useless to make generalizations. Many of the more important aspects of a community and a region are unique. For example:

San Francisco, California

The "City by the Bay" has a distinctive feature of geography. Since it is a peninsula, outward growth of the city itself is impossible. However, growth around the base of the peninsula has been substantial and, as prices rise, commuting distances increase as well.

With median housing prices in the city hovering at about $800,000, few people can afford even a modest 1,500-square-foot house in San Francisco. One demographic consequence of this high-priced situation is a decline in the number of families with children. The more likely buyer is a working couple with no children. In fact, in the decade from 1990 to 2000, according to U.S. Census data, the population grew by 3 percent. At the same time, the percentage of households in San Francisco with children declined from 21 percent down to 19 percent.

Changing demographics like this will ultimately affect the market both in terms of the types of properties that will be high in demand and quality-of-life issues like populations of school districts.

Albuquerque, New Mexico

Compared to other cities with a population of about 500,000 people, New Mexico's largest city falls short in many aspects. The median home price is $118,500— highly affordable by most people's standards. But local jobs are limited. Albuquerque is isolated in comparison to other metropolitan areas, which makes jobs more scarce as well. Unemployment is 5.3 percent compared to the national average of 4.8 percent. Median income is $38,272, or 9 percent lower than the national median of $41,994.

Because of these factors, prospects for growth in housing prices are slim in Albuquerque. There are no apparent driving forces, and the city is not a destination for large-scale tourism or retirement. For many, the mountain desert climate is not the most desirable compared to other places like the South and, notably, Florida. You will notice significant differences in economic trends and real estate prices between cities like Albuquerque and cities with larger satellite populations.

Detroit, Michigan

Few large cities in the United States have the profound demographic and economic problems of Detroit. Unemployment was at 7 percent as of early 2006, 46 percent higher than the national average. The city depends primarily on the Big Three auto markets headquartered in the immediate area. A decade ago, Detroit was termed the city most acutely vulnerable to economic cycles, due to its singular dependence on the auto industry. The situation is even worse today.

Detroit's problems are reflected in other ways. For example, it's ranked the second most dangerous city in the United States based on crime statistics, after Camden, New Jersey. Median income according to the U.S. Census was $14,717, or 65 percent under the national average. And the median home price as of the latest Census data was only $55,300.

These problems are only aggravated by the city's *falling* population over the past fifty years. From 1950 (pop. 1.8 million) to 2000 (950,000), Detroit's size ranking among U.S. cities went from fifth highest down to tenth highest. In this market, considering recent historical trends, any changes in auto industry employment rates are going to have a disastrous effect on the real estate market. Even if a housing boom should occur, this continuing vulnerability to a single industry makes Detroit one of the most troubling real estate regions in the United States.

Miami-Dade, Florida

Perhaps the best model for a residential property bubble is Miami Beach, Florida, and the surrounding area of Miami-Dade County. The city is relatively small, with a population of approximately 362,000. However, the county's population is over 2.2 million. Growth over the past century has been rapid: in 1900, fewer than 5,000 people lived in this region.

The housing market in the area does not operate as you would expect, given the other economic indicators. Miami

Beach's median income is $27,322, or 35 percent below the national average of $41,994. However, the median price of houses is $684,000 compared to the national average of $89,600. Dominating this real estate market are condos and, more specifically, rampant speculation in preconstruction.

Miami Beach is a study in economic contradiction: exceptionally high real estate prices (driven largely by the condo market), very low median income, and low unemployment (3.3 percent compared to the national average in early 2006 of 4.8 percent). But with condo prices of up to $34 million for prime beachfront locations, the Miami Beach region was in the middle of an ever-worsening pricing bubble by 2006.

The market was hot by the autumn of 2006. Numerous websites specializing in preconstruction sales had popped up. One such site (www.condoflip.com) downplays concerns about inflated prices with its slogan, "Bubbles are for bathtubs." Another site (www.kevintomlinson.com) specializes in both preconstruction buying and selling in Miami Beach.

But consider the actual statistics for this market: The number of *unsold* condos in and near Miami doubled from early 2005 to early 2006. As of 2006, 25,000 new condo units were under construction, and that was more than twice the number of condos purchased during the previous nine years. The demand, though, is mostly artificial. Local experts claim that three-fourths of the condo purchases in Miami are completed by speculators, with the intention of selling to other speculators once prices rise. This trend is driven by a 63 percent rise in condo market prices from 2002 to 2006. However, the more speculators in the market, the greater the price pressure and the more vulnerable the market becomes. Miami Beach was named one of the five locales in the United States most vulnerable to price correction.[1]

Miami-Dade is certainly a model for the housing bubble phenomenon. But the lesson to be learned from its status is that the same rules do not apply elsewhere, and its problems are not universal. It's the unique mix of local influences that created this bubble. When the south Florida condo speculation bubble bursts, the latest speculators will be stuck with overvalued properties, and the market will collapse. The mere fact that the number of units being built is equal to a nine-year supply tells the entire story. Because this particular brew of problems is occurring nowhere else in the world, the problems that Miami-Dade will eventually experience will not affect you. Bubbles do not burst everywhere at the same time or for the same reasons.

New York City

The average price for Manhattan residential two-bedroom homes was well over $1 million by 2004, and twice that for three or more bedrooms. Prices had risen more than 10 percent since the year before. If you ask anyone in New York, the housing bubble is alive and well. But with the largest population in the country and the highest population density, what is the future of New York?

With a city population over 8 million and metro area population over 22 million, New York City's housing situation is far more complex than most places. Restrictions on additional building, especially on the island of Manhattan, have driven prices high in recent years; but even with employment woes and the cyclical budget problems the city faces, it is not realistic to compare the New York "bubble" to the situation in southern Florida, where speculators are running prices higher each month. In the case of New York, many more economic and demographic factors have to be considered.

The 9/11 attacks affected the economy directly, but only temporarily. Employment trends in recent years include large-scale layoffs on Wall Street. For example, Merrill Lynch laid off one-fourth of its workforce (18,600 jobs) between 2001 and 2003. But that two-year period was post-9/11 and also involved the corporate scandals at Enron, WorldCom, and other companies. Large brokerage firms like Merrill Lynch were named in multiple lawsuits and paid fines to regulators for wrongdoing.

Since that period of time, New York's economy—including Wall Street—has returned to pre-2001 levels. So even with economic cycles in play, New York's market is complex and multifaceted. While many New Yorkers are convinced that they are in the middle of a real estate bubble, few are experiencing speculator-driven excesses like those in the Miami area. True, housing prices keep going up, but this is based mainly on the overall population growth, the steadily growing need for housing, and the number of available units, not on wild speculation in preconstruction properties that may never be occupied.

THE DIVERSITY OF REGIONAL MARKETS

Comparing San Francisco, Albuquerque, Detroit, Miami-Dade, and New York City demonstrates the diversity of regional markets. You can make similar comparisons with other cities or regions in the country and discover unique differences everywhere. As you make these comparisons, it becomes clear that the real estate cycle is regional in nature. It is reassuring to know that valuation of real estate in your community is not going to be affected by speculative activity thousands of miles away.

If you look to the stock market as a model, you get a somewhat exaggerated and inaccurate picture of how markets behave. The stock market, which is an auction market, is highly liquid and the daily buying and selling activity reflects trading ranges and millions of agreements between buyers and sellers. When markets are judged by indices, the effect of price changes on individual stocks is immediate and short term. For example, if the Dow Jones Industrial Average index falls 150 points in a single day, many stocks—perhaps most stocks—will fall as well. But this wrenching daily reaction to what are essentially false indices is highly technical (price-driven) and it normally reverses direction within a few days at most.

You cannot use the stock market as a model for real estate. One major reason is that real estate does not operate as an auction market. Another is that real estate is very illiquid compared to stocks. Finally, stock prices tend to operate without regard to regions at all, but real estate is nearly entirely regional in nature.

Unlike a stock, whose market value exists in the vapor of "the market," real estate's value is largely dependent on local factors. Property in midtown Manhattan is worth far more than grazing and shrub land in west Texas, for example. And it is not merely the use of land that defines its value; it is also the combination of regional factors at work that ultimately determine how much real estate is worth, how much the price changes, and whether change in price is rational or bubble-driven.

Defining the "Region"

It is essential to define a *region* in economic terms. This involves identification of commonality of economic and demographic features. For example, when you consider the alarming preconstruction condo bubble of Miami Beach, you probably need to encompass real estate values in the many surrounding towns and cities making up the Miami-Dade metropolitan area and perhaps all or most of Dade County, Florida. Does this region include other south Florida regions? The answers rely on what activities are going on in those communities. For example, if a preconstruction condo market is rife with speculation, then the same economic consequences will be suffered when the bubble bursts. If an identical set of demographic and economic factors make other southern Florida communities the same (in terms of employment, income, and population features) then it is likely that a bubble would affect the entire region.

Now consider a different example: Detroit. This city has numerous problems with crime, low income, depressed property values, and other poor trends. You may think of Detroit as a type of "reverse bubble"—a situation in which property values are artificially held down due to profound social and economic problems. What would happen if those problems were to disappear?

And how far would the outcome spread? In order to define Detroit, whose economic problems are tied unavoidably to the auto industry, you need to evaluate the range of area where employees reside. The Big Three auto manufacturers are located in Detroit (GM), Dearborn (Ford), and Auburn Hills (Daimler Chrysler). The greater Detroit area encompasses these communities, and it is a fair assumption that the majority of employees of the Big Three live within a 100-mile radius of the Detroit metropolitan area. So using the employment factor as a crucial one in determining value, the "region" should be defined based on those assumptions.

In the same vein, because the Boeing Company is one of the largest employers in the Seattle area, the Seattle region may be defined based on assumptions about Boeing's employment base. This is never entirely accurate, because employment is only one of many factors in regional property valuation. In Detroit, Seattle, and all other regions, distinct differences among cities and towns within an area demonstrate a broad range of price differences. But using the employment model as one aspect of defining a region certainly makes sense, to a degree.

Other Key Regional Characteristics

Beyond the employment-based regional definition, some areas are easier to define. Most people recognize the similarity of regional attributes to most metropolitan areas, where property investment is so often concentrated. A region may include the following additional distinctions:

1. *Common Employment Base and Commuter Patterns.* The definition of regions varies broadly from one place to another. Commuting distances into New York City expand far into Pennsylvania, Connecticut, New Jersey, and north to New York State communities. In comparison, the geographic commute region for Denver, Colorado, is more restricted. This is due to a

smaller economy, fewer people, and the geographic attributes of the area. Los Angeles includes a commute region that is exceptionally large, while, in comparison, San Francisco's commute region is far smaller (again, due partially to geography and partially to population differences).

2. *Population Characteristics by Age.* When you compare regions in terms of population makeup, you find distinct differences that also define the area. For example, cities and towns with large universities tend to have populations with relative low average age, while places like San Francisco report dwindling children population as prices have risen over the years. These types of differences clearly distinguish one region from another.

3. *Cultural and Traditional Uniqueness.* Most people are aware of numerous differences among regions in terms of heritage and culture. For example, the Minnesota and Dakota regions have higher than average percentages of Norwegian and Swedish families; Pennsylvania has areas dominated by those of German heritage. These factors often define regions as well. Places with larger numbers of immigrants further define regions or, within larger cities, distinguish neighborhoods from one another as well.

These concentrated population and cultural groups may inhibit real estate bubbles by maintaining their characteristics, if only by resisting outside development pressures.

4. *Proximity to Other Regions.* The region of some areas is defined by what is found nearby. For example, the portion of New Jersey in proximity to New York City (New York metropolitan area) can be defined partially as a commuter region for the city. By the same argument, areas surrounding San Francisco and Chicago are also commuter-based in character. Areas around Orlando, Florida, or Anaheim, California, are more accurately described as tourism-based.

5. *Shopping and Activity Centers.* The tourism of a region defines its economy and character; but in outlying areas, proxim-

ity to shopping and other activities also defines regions. In rural areas, satellite economies—those within rings of a central area— define regions in terms of shopping and activity-based regional character.

EXAMINING REGIONAL ECONOMIC FACTORS

The actual outcome of condo speculation in Florida will no doubt be disastrous for those last speculators who purchase units right before prices crash. But as long as the New York and San Francisco condo markets remain priced according to actual supply and demand realities, the effects will not be widespread—in spite of commonly held beliefs to the contrary.

Many people assume that there is but one real estate market, and that the bubble will burst everywhere at the same time. But that is not going to occur. If you examine a range of regional economic factors, you soon realize that local real estate trends respond to (and are at times caused by) local trends and are not particularly affected by national price changes or market conditions.

Here are some guidelines for analyzing your local market:

1. *Study price trends for the past five years.* Historically, average home prices rise over the long term. This is a potentially misleading statistic, because in any market, price trends look most promising immediately before a crash. So recent price movement should not serve as an indicator of where trends will move in the future. But the price trends over the past several years can give you a clearer picture of the regional market.

Because reported averages are just that, they are not reliable as indicators in your city or town. Just as the Dow Jones Industrial Average or the S&P 500 Index cannot be used to reliably predict where an individual stock's price will be next year, average home prices are equally unreliable. Even if you confine your study to regional home prices (the National Association of Realtors [NAR] and the U.S. Census Bureau both report regional price trends) you still don't know what your property values will be in a few years. Clearly, price differences in cities only a few miles apart may be subject to vastly different economic and demographic trends. So you really need to study price trends over at least a five-year period; but limit that study to prices in the immediate area and ignore regional and national averages.

2. *Collect regional economic information.* Where is the market heading? To develop a reliable estimate of how residential prices are likely to change in the near future, you need to also study those economic factors that are going to affect supply and demand directly. Is the local economy largely dependent on tourism, or is it a bedroom community for a large metropolitan area? Is it a college town? What future changes are likely to occur based on economic trends today? For example, if the area consists primarily of retirement-aged singles and couples, and little or no job market exists, what forces would cause future increases in property values? Compare this to a nearby city in which many jobs are found, the population is growing, and development is occurring in response to new residential demand.

3. *How much real estate is under construction today? How does this compare to recent population growth?* Many people overlook the trend in new construction, and base their assessment of real estate solely on current sales prices of homes. But this is a current and historical view only. Perhaps more revealing are two related trends: the number of new units currently being built, and the number of planned units not yet started.

If you limit your analysis of your local real estate market to existing units, you are not considering the impact of new housing that will be available within the next one to two years. If the population of your area is growing at twice the rate of new construction, property values are going to rise in the future. But if construction rates exceed the demand, a bubble has been created that will burst in the future. A prime example of this situation is the one described above in Miami Beach, where more condo units were being built than the total of nine years' sales.

4. *What are the employment and population trends?* Is the population growing or shrinking? Is the number of jobs in the region increasing or decreasing? The jobs market is probably the most reliable indicator of where real estate prices are headed. Ironically, speculators tend to look more to prices and development trends and ignore real demand elements. Developers are just as likely to be wrong about the market as speculators. For example, why would a developer invest in building *more* condo units in Miami Beach when the current number of available units exceeds the nine-year sales numbers? The population isn't increasing—in fact, the often-cited retiring baby boomers are not likely to have an effect, because the majority already own homes—but it is speculation that drives such markets. So in order to decide whether prices will rise or fall, it is more reliable to look at the population and job trends together, and to ignore the speculative short-term trends in real estate.

This is not a difficult comparison to make. A primary driver of population growth is the creation of new jobs. If employers are moving into an area and creating new jobs, people will follow. This places greater demand on housing. If there are going to be more families than new houses, it creates greater demand.

On the other hand, what does it mean when the opposite is going on? If local employers are shutting down operations and laying off employees, it means that people will be moving to find employment. That means that more homes will be for sale in the future. For example, in the Seattle area in 1971, layoffs took employment at Boeing from a high of 100,874 in 1967, down to 37,200. This caused a local recession through most of the 1970s and a big decline in housing prices. So many people were leaving the area that locals were known to say, "Will the last person to leave Seattle please turn off the lights." Seattle is typical of areas dependent on large employers or industry sectors (much like the

Detroit area). Downturns, cutbacks, and layoffs can have a disproportionate effect on the local population and, in turn, the local real estate market.

With this in mind, a study of employment and population trends should also include a critical view of dependence on companies and industries. Detroit and Seattle are examples of such potential problem areas. What happens to Detroit property values if General Motors lays off thousands? What happens in Seattle if Boeing goes through another of its cyclical recessions? It is not enough to study an area with historical trends in employment and population; it is also critical to evaluate the area's dependence issues.

For example, Seattle real estate prices rose in the 2004–2005 period, when median home prices went from $282,500 to $321,100. At the same time, the average number of days that properties were on the market fell, and active listings went down significantly, as shown below.[2] Collectively, these are very strong indicators for the real estate market:

	1st Quarter 2005	1st Quarter 2004
Seattle median home price	$321,100	$282,500
Average days on the market	53	65
Active listings	13,337	17,445

In the case of Seattle, the strength of the housing market is always related directly to the conditions of employment at Boeing. Does this mean Seattle was in a bubble by the end of 2005? It was, in one sense: The bubble was caused specifically by the employment cycles at Boeing, and history demonstrates this as well. When Boeing lays off thousands of people, it creates a local recession in housing prices and elsewhere. When Boeing begins hiring once again, housing prices rise.

5. *Look beyond price to review other important factors.* Looking only at prices is deceptive because it ignores the actual drivers of future real estate values—the kinds of activities that

cause bubbles. The specific factors that are going to determine future long-term real estate prices include the mix of population, climate, traffic, crime statistics, and economic drivers (such as tourism, or the mix of populations in the area).

The *mix of population* is going to include several groups. For example, communities may be dominated by retirement-age people, commuters, or college students. A mix of many different population groups is also likely, in which case you need to decide which group dominates the market. It is not enough to observe that a city's population rose by 20,000 people in two years if the bulk of that increase came from the expansion of a local university. Because college students are not likely to buy homes, the change in population will cause increased demand for rentals but have little direct impact on demand for owner-occupied housing.

Climate is also important in terms of the kinds of people who will want to live in an area. Florida and Arizona have been retirement destinations for decades and, recognizing this, developers have aggressively constructed housing/recreation communities in massive numbers. This trend has much to do with year-round warm weather in those states.

Traffic patterns emerge as a consequence of other trends. As prices rise for property in large cities, satellite communities move farther away and commuter levels grow. So traffic density increases along with pollution, delayed travel time, and noise. This affects property values directly, notably as commuter alternatives are sought and families are required to move farther away from city centers.

Crime statistics directly affect property values. As the rates of violent crimes grow, property values fall. Families move away so that actual demand declines significantly. High-crime areas like Camden, Newark, and Detroit report exceptionally low median housing prices and little if any increase over time. It is reasonable to assume that crime statistics in a region are going to directly affect housing prices as well.

An area's *primary economic centers* are also going to affect property values. The area around Orlando, Florida, has experienced significant growth in property values because of the expansive reach of Disney World and other destinations. For some areas dependent on tourism, the effect is highly seasonal. A very busy spring and summer season may be offset by dismal winter levels of activity, high unemployment, and a stand-still in property sales. While tourism may impact an area's housing market, offsetting conditions (like a tourism area that also boasts high employment levels) will counter this trend.

THE CLASSIC REAL ESTATE CYCLE

In the classic description of economic supply and demand, a simple model explains why prices rise and fall. As a real estate investor or homeowner, you may need a more complex model to help you understand the nature of real estate bubbles.

The basic model describes the local real estate cycle in the following "cause and effect" steps:

1. *Demand for real estate rises.* A starting point that is easily observed in the cycle is growth in demand for real estate. Symptoms of this include the obvious excess of buyers over sellers. When more people want property than there are properties for sale, that is clearly a strong sign that the cycle is entering an upswing.

Other symptoms of demand include the three basic market tests: time on the market, the price spread, and trends in local inventory. *Time on the market* is a test of how long it takes properties to sell. As the time on the market shrinks, it is a sign of growing demand; as it rises, it signifies reduced level of demand. The *price spread* is the percentage difference between the asked price and the final sales price. The lower the percentage, the stronger the market.

A third test is to watch *trends in the inventory* of properties available. If there is less than a six-month supply (calculated by dividing homes for sale by the average monthly completed sales), that is a healthy market; in fact, the six-month level is widely viewed as a point of equilibrium in the market. As you see the inventory declining, demand grows, and vice versa.

These tests—taken together with the observation of prices and the number of buyers—indicate the degree of demand and the change over time.

2. *Development follows demand.* When demand begins to rise, developers and contractors respond by increasing development activity. Your study of local conditions must include a review of current construction and planned construction, to estimate future trends. For example, the so-called preconstruction market for condos in Miami Beach demonstrates that the construction-unit-to-perceived-demand ratio is out of whack, which means the market is likely to fall apart at some point.

3. *Demand levels begin to slow down.* In an orderly market, demand simply is reduced over a period of time. In a bubble environment, it may occur quite suddenly, and speculators will find themselves holding overpriced and overvalued properties. However, even in a bubble real estate market, speculators are often able to spot the signs that the market is slowing down, simply by tracking the trends in time on the market, spread, and inventory, as well as noting the correlation of these demand factors to on-going and new construction.

4. *Supply exceeds demand.* Development of units tends to not slow down just because demand is itself slow. The tendency is to continue building new units as long as prices are rising. But eventually the demand stops. This may be due to a reversal in the demographic trend, sudden shifts in economics (jobs leaving the area), or simply the on-going trend in overconstruction. Because no two real estate cycles are the same in terms of duration, this phase seems to always take everyone by surprise, especially developers and speculators.

5. *Development activity slows or stops.* When supply overtakes demand levels, developers tend to either slow down or stop

altogether. Their prices for properties are often based on the assumption that ever-growing price trends will continue indefinitely. When prices become soft and flatten out or fall, development itself eventually stops altogether.

6. *Demand ceases and the market hits bottom.* At the bottom of the cycle, demand reaches all-time low levels due to oversupply. This is the end of the demand-supply cycle and the beginning of a new one. Price levels at this point are not necessarily the same as at the beginning of the cycle. When growth trends rise over time, the end of one cycle may include price levels above previous prices. But in the case of a severe real estate bubble, market prices may fall far below those levels at the beginning of the "bubble cycle." This occurs because the rise in prices was driven by speculation, reduced interest rates, and other short-term causes. The remaining long-term influences on the real estate cycle—which always go back to actual economic supply and demand—may lag several years behind the short-term influences of noneconomic factors.

A summary of the traditional supply-and-demand cycle is illustrated in Figure 2-1.

This typical supply-and-demand cycle involves gradual change. Note also that price, the major determinant in the economic "health" of the real estate market, follows the actual economic changes. Even as supply softens, for example, the momentum of price growth is likely to continue, fueled by buyer enthusiasm and speculation. An extreme case (such as Miami Beach) involves developers and speculators apparently oblivious to the signs that the market peaked and that the bubble is likely to burst at any moment.

THE BUBBLE-DRIVEN REAL ESTATE CYCLE

In a bubble-driven real estate cycle, economic supply and demand is buried under the price growth and decline caused by

Figure 2-1. Traditional supply and demand cycle.

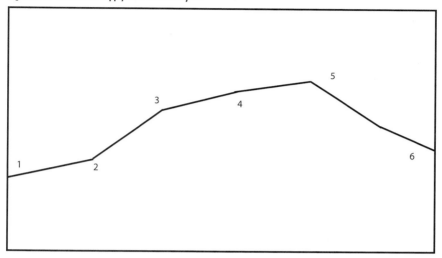

1 Demand for real estate rises.
2 Development follows demand.
3 Demand levels begin to slow down.
4 Supply exceeds demand.
5 Development activity slows or stops.
6 Demand ceases and the market hits bottom.

other factors. Figure 2-2 is a revised look at the real estate cycle when the trend is bubble-driven.

In this variation of the cycle, the changes are more extreme and, in terms of time, may also be more sudden. For example, when the bubble bursts (at phases 5 and 6) prices tend to fall drastically and suddenly. This is when speculators find themselves holding overpriced properties and are taken by surprise.

Supply-and-demand cycles do not happen spontaneously or without cause. Every change in price is the logical result of specific events and a series of previous changes. So as long as the property you own is well priced and demand levels are reasonable, you will not need to worry about the real estate bubble. But if your property's value has increased in recent months or years and the levels of growth make no sense to you, you may experience a correction in the future. This is especially true if the growth in prices was the result of speculation and other forms of artificial short-term demand.

Figure 2-2. Bubble-driven real estate cycle.

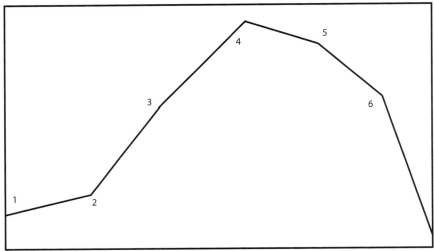

1 Demand for real estate rises.
2 Development follows demand.
3 Demand levels begin to slow down.
4 Supply exceeds demand.
5 Development activity slows or stops.
6 Demand ceases and the market hits bottom.

Given the fact that the causes of market bubbles are well known, they can also be anticipated. What you cannot anticipate is the precise timing of cyclical changes. But it is useful to evaluate real estate on locally based models, taking into account the current trends and activity underway in real estate development.

A supply-side example should include a study of the current residential market and the number of housing units that are:

1. Existing

2. Under construction

3. Planned

Second, you need to analyze the population trends. Are people moving to the area and if so, how many per year? How does this trend compare to the number of housing markets existing and planned? This comparison tells the "supply-side" story fairly accurately, even though it is based on recent historical trends. If you estimate how those trends are going to continue into the future, you identify the influences on real estate prices that come from the supply side.

A demand-side example includes some of the same data, but from a different perspective. If you remember that development tends to outpace actual demand, you can critically analyze how and when housing units are being planned and built. To return to the classic bubble example, the number of condo units being constructed by 2006 in Miami Beach was a case of lunacy. Any outsider could see the glaring excess in investing in construction of supply exceeding nine years' worth of demand. But when prices are going up, those with cash on the line tend to be blind to the realities. They actually come to believe that "bubbles are for bathtubs," and they argue against the problems of overpriced housing units. A study of demand-driven cyclical trends demonstrates the two important factors in bubble-driven environments: the "greed factor" and the "greater-fool theory."

The *greed factor* is a tendency to want to get into a market because prices are rising. For speculators, the profits earned are never enough. Once they double the capital invested, they are likely to put those profits back in and to buy two units, then five, then ten . . . and ultimately they'll have thousands of dollars in paper profits that will evaporate overnight when the bubble bursts.

The *greater-fool theory* tells speculators that, even though they are paying more than the property is actually worth, a greater fool will be available in a few months to pay an even higher price. Eventually, the greater fool—the last person to put money into a property—gets stuck with the overpriced deal and loses everything. But this is not necessarily a new speculator. The tendency (remember the greed factor) is for speculators to want to parlay their early modest profits into ever-larger profits. So in a sense, the greed factor works to make today's sucker tomorrow's greater fool.

In a true economic analysis, demand is recognized as being the result of actual, tangible causes. These include incoming jobs and migration of people. For example, in the San Francisco Bay Area, the late 1980s price boom in the north, east, and south Bay areas was a direct result of major employers leaving San Francisco to relocate to the suburbs. This was a response to an ill-conceived city payroll tax. Employers recognized the high cost of this tax and responded by moving their large employee base to other counties. As a consequence, the *real* demand for housing—a result of people relocating out of San Francisco—created rapid increases in housing prices. Even though the price changes were rapid, they were not bubble-driven. There were actual economic causes for the change.

ANTICIPATING REGIONAL CHANGE

Regional characteristics—like most aspects of real estate—are not always set in stone. They change as population shifts occur, highways are rerouted, and employers relocate. You need to be able to anticipate possible changes to identify:

1. Whether you are in a bubble or a developing bubble

2. Potential investment bargains

3. Likely future changes in value based on economics and the traditional supply and demand cycle

You spot regional emerging trends by watching the local attributes affecting real estate: changes in employment levels (plus or minus), new housing starts, and any outside influences on the local economy (relocation of employer facilities, closures of existing facilities, plans for new recreational sites). These trends can then be compared to price trends in local residential markets to try and spot whether changes are likely to occur, and in which direction. If you live in an area where prices have risen far more rapidly than you can justify based on identifiable economic and demographic causes, your region might be in a real estate bubble.

How severe is the bubble? Some areas (such as, again, Miami Beach) may be extreme, others only mild. Additionally, the bubble may refer specifically to only one type of real estate. If all of the activity involves the condo market, how does that affect other property? Of course, if the market were to realize that many more condo units had been built than demand can meet for the coming decade, the effects will be seen in single-family housing as well, although not as severely.

The recessionary effects of a bubble bursting will also affect the overall regional economy. When Boeing laid off tens of thousands of workers in the early 1970s, Seattle's economy experienced a ten-year recession. Every job creates, indirectly, as many as three to five additional jobs in support industries. So as new jobs are created in a region, it translates to a multiple of higher employment; if employers leave an area, the same statistical reality applies in the opposite direction.

In judging the kinds of changes likely to occur in your region, avoid using national averages as definitive indicators of what is likely to occur in the future. The overall trends—normally providing you with little more than average housing prices—may be broken down by broad regions (the Northeast, the Northwest, the South, the Southwest, etc.) but these are not "regions" for the purpose of your analysis. The regions as defined by the Census Bureau and the NAR are only geographical distinctions of the entire country; but the statistics provided on this level are virtually useless in your regional tests of real estate values.

As demonstrated in this chapter, a region may be quite narrowly defined. It may consist of a single county or city. Within one area, regional impact may involve only a slice of the market (such as the preconstruction condo market). So when you are analyzing property in Miami-Dade, national price statistics for "eastern United States" are useless. National price statistics are quite valuable for judging the overall health of the real estate market and of investment values on a broad scale, but they tell you absolutely nothing about a particular region. You need to narrow down the actual region in terms of local economic forces, demographics, and the recent price history for that region—not the price trends in national "regions" found in overall statistical summaries.

It is not enough to simply look at prices and price trends to decide whether homes are affordable. Chapter 3 examines the larger economic impacts on real estate bubbles.

NOTES

1. Stephane Fitch, "The Last Speculators," *Forbes*, March 27, 2006.
2. Maura Webber Sadovi, "Seattle Housing Market Remains Strong," *Real Estate Journal (Wall Street Journal)*, July 6, 2005.

Stocks, Bonds, Real Estate, and Money

Many investors tend to think about real estate completely separately from the stock market and, in fact, from the economy itself. When you hear about monetary policy, trade deficits, and inflation, you may not equate those economic trends with the value of real estate or with the consequences of real estate bubbles. But the whole economic situation is tied together. Real estate is a very important part of the overall economy and it cannot be isolated from the larger picture.

The financial press tries to simplify real estate pricing. Writers look for items that can be summarized in three short paragraphs and explained for an audience that is not interested in any in-depth analysis. Television and radio journalism is even worse when it comes to simplifying complex ideas. The usual sound bite summarizes the market by reporting the percentage rise in national average home prices last year, an increased foreclosure rate, or fears about interest rate hikes. All of these news items are important, but they are only a small piece of a much larger and more complicated story.

HOW REAL ESTATE FITS YOUR FINANCIAL PLAN

Among the simplifications you hear in the media is the idea that people invest either in stocks or bonds, or in stocks or real estate. The picture being painted is one of massive numbers of investors taking money out of one market and placing all of it in another. But the interaction among these large markets is not quite as simple as it is portrayed. Just as the media gets the most mileage out of describing real estate bubbles as existing everywhere, they also simplify the overall economy by distorting the interactions among markets.

If you ignore the many minor market segments and focus on just three—real estate, stocks, and bonds—it becomes clear that whereas these coexist and affect each other, they also are affected by many outside influences. For example, international exchange rates and trade deficits affect the health of the U.S. economy and, potentially, the way that businesses operate. This may ultimately translate into gains or losses in the labor market, which also affect interest rates and housing values. The interdependence of markets is only one aspect of the big picture; another is the way in which each market is also affected by nonmarket and noninvestment forces.

Asset Allocation

Asset allocation is the process of dividing investment capital among different markets. The purpose is to spread your risks around so that no single economic influence or market change affects your entire portfolio. For example, you might allocate your investment capital one-third each to real estate, stocks, and bonds. Based on how those markets change and how economic conditions emerge, you might decide to give more or less weight to any of these allocation centers.

However, allocation is not a magic formula that can solve the problems of investing your capital. Your financial situation, risk tolerance, income, and assets differ from everyone else's. You may experience larger or smaller liquidity requirements in your portfolio than your neighbor, for example. You cannot rely on published asset allocation recommendations provided to you without considering your overall financial situation.

There is a tendency to oversimplify the process of allocation by classifying everyone into a few simple groups. For example, UBS offers five asset-allocation-based mutual funds, designed for the following groups:

Fixed income	100% bonds
Yield	75% bonds; 25% stocks
Balanced	50% bonds and money market; 50% stocks
Growth	25% bonds; 75% stocks
Equity	100% stocks[1]

This rather obvious division into 25-percent increments emphasizes only the areas mutual fund managers understand: stocks and bonds. And even if your risk profile mandates that none of your assets should be in real estate, these formulated fund groups do not necessarily fit your exact needs. These asset allocation funds demonstrate the assumption—seen too often in the stock market—that every investor can be fit into one of five classifications.

The life changes that everyone experiences are not easily classified into one of five groupings, however. Imagine how important events in your life—marriage, buying your first home, the birth of a child, starting a new career, or the death of a loved one, for example—drastically affect your financial plan. Single people beginning their careers have far different risk profiles from a married couple with two children and a mortgage, or from a retired couple living on a fixed income.

Important changes make subtle differences in a range of financial requirements: liquidity, insurance of many kinds, retirement planning, saving for college education of a child, and so many other considerations. The methods you use in allocating assets also will vary based on your personal experience.

Your Home as an Investment

Mutual fund advisors tend to ignore the question of where real estate fits with your long-term financial planning and to focus on the capital you have available to invest. But your home is an investment as well.

If you have placed $40,000 as a down payment on your home and you have an additional $40,000 in stocks plus $20,000 in an income-focused mutual fund (consisting mostly of bonds), how are your assets allocated? Most stock market people would say you were 80/20 in stocks and bonds. But to be more accurate, you are 40/40/20 in real estate, stocks, and bonds. This changes *everything* about how you have allocated your resources.

This is not merely an exercise in definition: The inclusion of real estate defines your portfolio accurately, even if it involves your primary residence and no outside investments.

Planning Ahead

Of course, if you subscribe to the theory that the housing market all over the country is going to collapse, then you should sell your home immediately, rent a house, and wait out the big crash. This actually is the belief expressed by one financial consultant, who warns, "It's gonna be bad for housing. It's a real threat to everything."[2]

Obviously, there are disputes and disagreements about the extent of a bubble and its ramifications when prices fall (whether locally or everywhere). The exact opposite view of real estate bubbles is expressed by David Lereah, the chief economist of the National Association of Realtors (NAR), who explains, "A bubble is the wrong image. I think a balloon is a much better image. It expands and contracts as air goes in and out, but it maintains its integrity."[3]

In this book, the point of view is somewhere between these two extremes. The point here is that the bubble will not burst everywhere due to the regional character of the real estate market. However, some areas will experience a serious correction in real estate due to excess speculation and price increases. In considering how to plan ahead with the larger economy in mind, your point of view about real estate should affect where and how you invest capital. There are no formulas for allocation that work universally; you need to study the question and determine how to proceed based on your experience and knowledge, willingness to assume risks, income and assets, age, and financial situation.

THE EVOLUTION OF THE SECONDARY MARKET

A half-century ago, home ownership was far different from what it is today. People visited their local bank and loans were approved. There was a limit to how much money a lender could place into mortgages, because each lender's reserves set limits on its debt levels.

That has all changed. Today, almost everyone who owns real estate has the majority of the purchase price financed on the "secondary market."

The majority of commercial loans are underwritten by mortgage companies, banks, and savings institutions. but these loans are then sold on the secondary market and packaged in mortgage pools. Shares of those pools are sold to investors. This has become the modern way that mortgage loans are financed, by mortgage pools rather than through lenders' reserves. Of course, this secondary market has vastly expanded the money supply available for mortgage loans.

The lenders continue to service loans that are sold to the secondary market, so the sale of the actual liability is invisible to the borrower. The lender receives a fee for collecting mortgage payments, chasing down delinquencies, and collecting and paying impounds. But the liability itself is no longer limited to a lender's reserves. Even a small lender (as measured by assets) can write a nice volume of mortgage loans without tying up its reserves for thirty years.

Fannie Mae

The big change began in 1968. The Federal National Mortgage Association (FNMA, or "Fannie Mae") was privatized and its role expanded to allow the company to buy mortgages from commercial lenders. Originally formed in 1938 during the New Deal era, Fannie Mae (www.fnma.com) is now a shareholder-owned private corporation traded on the New York Stock Exchange (NYSE:FNM) and part of the S&P 500 Composite Stock Price Index.

The congressional charter that set up Fannie Mae as a private corporation allows the corporation to expand mortgage lending. As the corporation itself explains, it does not lend money directly to borrowers, but "works with lenders to make sure they don't run out of mortgage funds."[4]

Ginnie Mae

In the same year (1968), the Government National Mortgage Association (GNMA, or "Ginnie Mae") began participating in the secondary market as well. This is a quasi-government organization that guarantees loans insured by the FHA, the VA, Rural Housing Service (RHS), HUD, and other agencies.

Ginnie Mae provides two distinct products: *Mortgage-Backed Securities* (MBS) are mortgage pools issued by lenders and acquired by Ginnie Mae. The pools created by placing individual loans into security products are guaranteed by the "full faith and credit" of the U.S. government, which is recognized as the best form of security available on any investment. The vast majority of Ginnie Mae mortgages come from mortgage bankers (69 percent), and another 23 percent come from commercial banks and savings and loans. The remainder are from credit unions, mutual savings banks, and other lenders.

Ginnie Mae also issues *Real Estate Mortgage Investment Conduits* (REMICs), which collect mortgages into pools. Instead of selling shares directly to investors, REMIC shares are marketed much like bonds, with specified maturity dates and varying levels of seniority.

Freddie Mac

A third important member of the secondary market is the Federal Home Loan Mortgage Corporation (FHLMC, or "Freddie Mac"). Freddie Mac was chartered by the U.S. government in 1970 to buy mortgages from lenders, pool them together, and then sell shares to investors, like its competitor Fannie Mae.

The MBS Freddie Mac issues and markets become debt securities that, like bonds, have maturities and repayment guarantees. This is possible because the pools formed are based on secured debts in the form of mortgages. The company participates in the MBS market and also issues debt securities in exchange for directly purchased mortgage loans that are not placed into investment pools. These mortgage payments are collected and directed by Freddie Mac, and financed through issuance of debt securities. Those securities are sold to investors. The distinction between the two formats is this: Investors can purchase shares in mortgage pools consisting of many secured mortgages, or they can purchase debt securities from Freddie Mac to fund the company's direct ownership of mortgages.

Cash, Liquidity, and Debt

The three secondary market organizations together have over $3.6 *trillion* in purchased loans and loan guarantees, which is 65 percent of the massive $5.7 trillion residential mortgage market. These staggering numbers equal many multiples of the secondary market equity. To illustrate this point, consider the following comparisons:

In Billions of Dollars

Organization	Stockholders' Equity	Mortgage Guarantees	Mortgages on the books
Fannie Mae	$15.0	$751.4	$990.4
Freddie Mac	17.6	519.0	725.0
Ginnie Mae	8.1	5.7	604.0[5]

These relative dollar values are graphically illustrated in Figure 3-1.

The secondary market has brought tremendous liquidity into the housing market. In fact, without these organizations, the extent of growth in mortgage activity would have placed a strain on the traditional reserve bank system. This limitation may have prevented the kinds of growth the country has experienced. However, the organizations do not seem to be organized along the same lines as traditional stock corporations. If you think of the combination of stockholders' equity and debt (both carried

Figure 3-1. Equity and debt in the U.S. secondary market (in billions of dollars).

Equity and debt in the secondary market (in billions of dollars)

Source: Fannie Mae, Freddie Mac, and Ginnie Mae annual reports.

and guaranteed) as overall capitalization, these three secondary market companies are largely made up of debt. Very little equity even exists.

Real estate bubbles place great risk in the secondary market. Even without a vast increase in foreclosures, the secondary market carries the majority of all mortgage debt: 65 percent. So if there were to be a massive, nationwide bubble burst, how would these loan guarantees hold up? With so little equity value—about 1 percent of total capitalization—stockholder value (in Freddie Mac and Fannie Mae) would certainly fall, but the real losses would fall on loan guarantees made, ultimately, by the federal government.

A "universal" bubble burst is unlikely because equity in the residential market does cover most of the current debt levels. But the analysis between loan guarantees versus stockholders' equity demonstrates that the secondary market is far from typical in terms of how most corporations are formed. The mortgage market is based on debt and guarantees, with very little actual equity backing it up. To the extent that investors buy shares in mortgage pools created by the secondary market organizations, this debt level is disbursed and financed by the market.

In analyzing the state of the real estate market—and specifically how it is affected by bubbles and the risk exposure of the secondary market—the following observations can be made:

1. The level of debt and loan guarantees has expanded rapidly in recent decades.

2. Some fallout is likely in the secondary market when bubbles burst in larger loan-intensive regions.

3. Because the debt is spread throughout the debt market mostly through mortgage pools, the risks are also spread around.

4. Because bubbles are regional in nature, even a large burst would have some ripple effect to other areas. But a wide-

spread burst is not likely because the existing mortgage debt—as large as it is—represents coverage of significant equity.

THE CURRENT REAL ESTATE MARKET

Today's real estate market has evolved over many decades and has been affected by far more than mere supply and demand. Economic and monetary policy, the emergence of a secondary market for mortgage loans, and cyclical changes in interest rates have all contributed to real estate bubbles and an acceleration in the real estate cycle. But there are a few other things to take into consideration if you want to better understand the rise of bubbles in today's market.

Declining Value of the Dollar

Economists will tell you that *real* market value has to be compared in terms of the spending power of money. So if the dollar's spending power has declined, do higher real estate prices even matter? In one respect, higher prices simply mean you need more dollars to buy the same property. So to some degree, reduced spending power does have to be taken into account when making judgments about real estate bubbles. Everyone has heard a story about a house in their community that sold for $30,000 back in 1970 and is on the market today for $450,000. But even though spending power does change, does it matter today? A look back reveals that some increases in market value reflect reduced spending power, accompanied by real growth in demand. This real growth is reflected in the U.S. population trend.

Population Growth

In 1970, the number of people living in the United States was two-thirds the number estimated by 2010. This change represents real demand. Will the growth in demand continue? A look at the U.S. population suggests that it will. In 1900, only 76 million people lived in the United States, live expectancy was about 40, and most people never traveled more than 20 miles from their birthplace. The economy was largely agricultural, and the concept of retirement was unheard of. Today, approximately 300 million people—a growth of 400 percent—live in the United States, and life expectancy is in the mid-70s. The economy is varied but far from agriculturally dominated, and most people expect to enjoy two or more decades of retirement. Figure 3-2 illustrates the growth in population over the past century.

Behind the Raw Numbers

Once you discount a real estate bubble (reflected in the prices of residential real estate) by the declining purchasing power of the dollar and by the growing population, you realize that the bubble—even in the most extreme cases—is not as severe as it might seem if you looked at only the raw numbers. In some areas, the actual changes in real estate have only kept pace with inflation, which means that in spite of the increased prices there has been little or no real change in the market.

The decline in spending power of the dollar is worth further examination. For example, today's dollar buys one-half of what it bought only twenty years ago. Figure 3-3 shows that the purchasing power of the U.S. dollar has fallen by nearly one-half in the years from 1984 through 2004.

If the cost of a house today is twice of what the same house cost in 1984, there has not been any real change. It is not accurate to say that property values have grown. A 1984 purchase for $125,000 (in 1984 dollars) is the same as the purchase of a $250,000 house (in 2004 dollars, with only one-half the purchasing power of 1984). This is merely the effect of inflation, which can be looked at in two ways. First, you can define inflation as "higher prices." Second, you can assume that prices have not changed, but the purchasing power of the dollar has declined. In

Figure 3-2. U.S. population growth: 1900 to 2010.

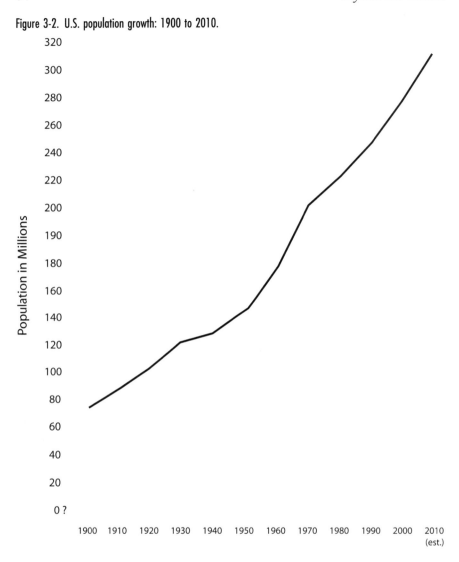

fact, these are just two different ways of defining the same change in value over time.

Artificial Equity

Many people blame real estate bubbles on historically low interest rates. The official policy expressed by the Federal Reserve has always been that lower rates spark greater economic produc-

Figure 3-3. Purchasing power of U.S. dollar: 1984 to 2004.

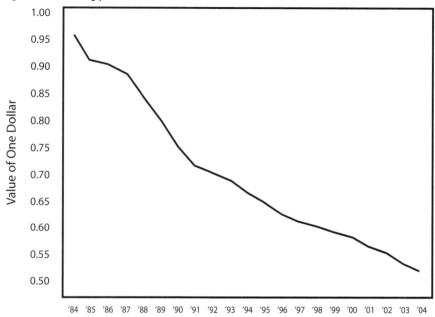

Source: U.S. Bureau of Labor Statistics.

tivity, expansion, and investment in plant and equipment. This is a fine model, but since the mid-1990s the low interest rates have not led to greater manufacturing capacity. They have led to an expansion of mortgage debt.

When bubbles do exist, higher home equity is an illusion. Although real demand exists and has existed for many decades—as shown by growth in the population alone—there is a degree of artificial growth as well, more in some regions than in others. This "fake equity" is the most vulnerable and will be likely to evaporate when the bubble bursts.

THE ECONOMIC CHANGES OF THE 1970s

Several things began to occur in the 1970s that affect today's housing prices and the regional bubbles seen around the country. On August 15, 1971, President Richard Nixon removed U.S.

currency from the gold standard. Before that date, the printing of money was restricted by actual gold reserves. So if more currency was printed than the country had in actual gold, it was not backed up. But since 1971, the whole system of money was changed and the government freed itself to print all the money it wanted, within its own monetary policies. This affected real estate valuation, notably because of changes on the lending side.

For the mortgage lending business, this change meant that there was really no limit on how much money could be loaned out. In today's system of money not backed up by gold, the Federal Reserve is limited only by its supplies of paper and ink, and there is no link to gold reserves. So the "money supply" is no longer defined by the amount of gold stored in a secure vault in Fort Knox. Lenders, working through the secondary market, can create all the mortgage loans they want. This has profoundly redefined the way that homes are bought and sold. It also has affected interest rate policies.

From 2001 to 2005, when rates fell below previously established low levels, mortgage loans expanded without limit—and that lack of limit was a direct outcome of the 1971 decision to abandon the gold standard. Today, U.S. money is no longer called "silver certificates." Now the wording on paper money reads "Federal Reserve note." It is not money in the real sense, but an IOU.

Birth of the Bubbles

Today's proliferation of real estate bubbles—like so many variations of bubbles throughout the economy—was encouraged at least partially by the decision made back in 1971. It is interesting to speculate about what would have happened if President Nixon had not removed the U.S. currency from the gold standard. Up until that time, gold was worth $35 per ounce, by law. If, instead of doing away with the gold standard, this price restriction had been removed, it would have placed gold's value on the open market.

This option was not considered a good idea. It would have signaled other countries to raise their prices on goods exported to the United States. For example, removing the price restriction on gold would have led to Germany raising its export price to 2.4 times above 1971 prices, while U.S. goods would have continued selling in Germany for 41 percent of prior levels.[6]

So even though the government had economic reasons for the decision, the new monetary environment effectively started the ball rolling on today's real estate bubbles. The unintended consequences thirty-five years later include not only distorted real estate values in many communities, but a complete reversal of the U.S. position in the world economy. In 1971, the U.S. dollar was strong and rising compared to the currencies of other nations. Today, the dollar has been devalued and continues to fall. So, going back to the analysis of lost purchasing power, it remains important to understand that higher real estate prices contain at least three elements:

- Real demand created by a growing population
- Adjustments for reduced purchasing power of the dollar
- Actual bubbles created by artificial demand

These three elements work together and are difficult to separate in any specific market. It is important to be aware of all three influences on real estate prices. But how much does each contribute to prices in your city?

Further Changes

The economic changes that began in 1971 continued, further affecting the open economy for all commodities, including real estate. President Nixon instituted wage and price controls in 1971 and when these didn't work, they were canceled—only to be tried again after the 1972 election; these were again canceled in 1974 when it became evident that these government controls did nothing to curb inflation. In fact, the move seemed only to make inflation worse.

Another consequence of abandoning the gold standard was that it destroyed a system that had been in place since the end of World War II, the Bretton Woods system (named for the location in New Hampshire of the U.N. Monetary and Financial Conference of July 1944). At that conference the International Monetary Fund (IMF) was formed. This organization was set up to regulate and control currency values, and to operate as an international monetary policymaking body.

Also established at the Bretton Woods conference was the International Bank for Reconstruction and Development (known as The World Bank). Its purpose was to provide loans to countries whose infrastructure had been destroyed during the war.

Both of the major organizations founded as part of this international conference evolved beyond their original purpose, providing financial aid to many developing nations around the world. The agreement brought order to international monetary policy and curtailed exchange rate fluctuations that would otherwise jeopardize a country's solvency or ability to trade. The system worked well up until 1971.

The decision by President Nixon that year to remove U.S. currency from the gold standard contradicted the orderly international monetary controls created by Bretton Woods. Many years after the original purpose of rebuilding countries after the war had passed, the system continued to provide stability in the international economy, but the U.S. decision made much of this effort ineffectual.

STOCKS AND REAL ESTATE BUBBLES

Bubbles occur continuously in all markets, to one degree or another. You can learn a lot about how real estate bubbles are likely to evolve by observing behavior on the stock market. When a large run-up in prices occurs across a broad spectrum of the market (meaning most stocks follow the trend) a reversal of fortunes eventually takes place. Most stocks rise during the price run-up, and most stocks fall when the trend turns around. An interesting, longer-term effect also occurs, however.

Long-Term Trends

If companies are well managed and profitable, the short-term gyrations of the stock market affect prices temporarily, but over time each company establishes its own trend. In the real estate market, the same tendency usually rules. For example, if the underlying economic and demographic indicators are strong and demand for housing is growing, then price levels are going to grow as well. Bubbles may cause prices to outpace actual demand and, upon correction, those prices will retreat temporarily. But they will rebound if, in fact, the trend is based on real demand and not just price frenzy.

Prices react in the short term but long-term trends eventually win. There is a tendency to believe that real estate operates on some level other than the stock market, that these two operate differently or react to economic events differently, and that a real estate bubble is different from a stock market bubble.

Short-Term Influences

After Hurricane Katrina hit New Orleans, many families relocated to Shreveport, other Louisiana cities, and far beyond. Real estate prices shot up immediately due to the sudden demand. After a few months, prices came down somewhat. The point remains, however, that the short-term impact was caused by an unusual event.

A similar impact has been experienced in San Francisco, not once but several times. From the Gold Rush of 1849, San Francisco grew rapidly and became a major destination and business center where, previously, almost no one lived. By 1906, the population of 400,000 had created real demand for real estate. The earthquake destroyed large sections of the city and, for several years, real estate prices were depressed. They rebounded by 1915, however, and citizens forgot about the impact of the devastation.

A similar effect was seen in San Francisco in 1989. In the previous two years, real estate values had been rising rapidly in the entire Bay Area. During the year following the 1989 earthquake, property values fell, but they came back and the growing price trend caught up and even exceeded previous levels. One local writer explained the San Francisco real estate trend:

> There is simply no empirical information that proves that real-estate values fall (in the mid- to long-term) after earthquakes or are even devalued in earthquake-prone locations. For whatever reason, the market makes no apparent adjustments for earthquake risks or, for that matter, hurricane risks. In fact, the opposite might be true.[7]

By observing how short-term influences affect real estate markets (including events like hurricanes and earthquakes), it is reasonable to conclude that the real estate market acts a lot like the stock market.

Stock Market Bubbles

If you think about how bubbles actually work in the stock market, you get a pretty accurate picture. And remember, too, that bubbles work in both price increases and price decreases. The example of San Francisco following major earthquakes makes this point.

In the stock market, sudden price changes (upward or downward) *always* end up stopping and reversing at some point, usually sooner rather than later. In severe downward trends like the 1929 market crash, it takes several years for the reversal to occur. More typically, the trend turns around quite rapidly. In 1987, the biggest one-day market crash in history occurred. On

October 19, 1987, the Dow Jones Industrial Average fell 508 points, or 22.6 percent, a loss of value greater than $500 billion. Less than one year later, the market had fully recovered.

This biggest-ever drop in the stock market can be viewed as the crash of a stock market bubble. In looking back, endless analysis can identify various causes for the decline, but for real estate investors a single observation is worth making: The market-wide crash affected prices for less than one year. This means that even the biggest bubble does not affect real demand and real supply. Short-term price declines self-correct in most cases and in the short term.

Bubbles can go in both directions. Another way to view the 1987 crash in the stock market is that the massive price drop was a downward price bubble. That downward bubble burst within one year and prices returned to normal levels. The suggestion that bubbles move in both directions is not merely an intellectualized way to look at falling prices; it is realistic. All markets rise and then fall cyclically, and all markets fall and then rise. This is simply the way trends operate, so "bubbles" can be observed in upward or downward price trends. But while bubbles tend to be short term in nature (at least in the stock market), they do not affect longer-term price trends, which are always dominated by real supply and demand.

Real Estate Bubbles

The real estate market is extremely illiquid compared to the stock market. This disparity in the methods of buying and selling between residences and shares of stock also means that bubbles are not likely to be identical in duration. Stock market price changes can be seen on daily and weekly trends. Real estate prices tend to move in a slower cyclical pattern. So whereas stock market bubbles in either direction may reverse within less than one year, the slower-moving real estate cycle may require a longer period for recovery. Thus, in an area where prices have risen due to combined real demand and a degree of bubble demand, a burst bubble is likely to keep prices down for longer than you would experience in the stock market. Some points to keep in mind in observing these differences:

1. *Only speculators should anticipate short-term price trends in real estate.* The likelihood that today's high prices may fall rapidly in the future is a concern for property flippers and players in the preconstruction market. But homeowners cannot escape the cycle. If you sell your house today, you have to buy a house somewhere else. So trying to time a decision to sell your property is not advisable because—as a homeowner—you should be far more interested in long-term value, affordability of your mortgage, and your family's security. Investment return is a secondary motive.

2. *Continuing to study your local economic and demographic trends is wiser than reacting to a bubble economy.* As long as you believe that local supply and demand are at realistic levels within a predictable real estate cycle, there should be no reason to be concerned about the real estate bubble. Keep an eye on economic trends (interest rates, for example) and demographic trends (population, employment) to determine the relative health of your local real estate market.

If you believe interest rates are rising, you may want to replace a variable-rate mortgage with a long-term fixed-rate mortgage. If you believe that economic and demographic trends are weakening, it does not mean you need to sell your home. Base your point of view on your original purchase price, interest rate, monthly payment on your mortgage, and the desirability of living there. If you can afford your payments, your family is comfortable and safe, and you would like to stay where you are for many years to come, you can afford to ignore short-term cyclical changes in prices.

3. *If you do conclude that the main driver of prices in your region are not real, sell before the bubble bursts.* There

is no justification for a universal call to get out of real estate now. Some books and articles have claimed that the bubble is going to burst everywhere and prices are going to fall across the entire geographic spectrum. As stated earlier, this does not make sense. However, if you conclude that the price of real estate you own is unrealistically inflated, it makes sense to sell now and take out the equity, move somewhere else, and invest in a region where real estate prices reflect real supply and demand. Just as you would sell shares of stock whose price had run up to unexpected new high levels (called "profit-taking") you can also take profits on real estate, but this is only appropriate if and when you see trouble in the form of extreme price run-up due to a bubble.

Also, remember that a price trend is likely to consist of real demand as well as a degree of bubble demand. Therefore, it is not necessarily clear that the recent price changes are caused by one or the other. The combined causes are more likely, making identification difficult. If there is a glaring price run-up that simply makes no sense, however, it means you are probably in the middle of a real estate bubble. In extreme cases it is far easier to identify the problem. Just as a stock market investor knows when stock prices are high—because it is so obvious—the same rule applies to real estate. But so many investors and speculators seem to ignore the bubble effect in property values, convinced that prices must continue rising indefinitely.

ARTIFICIAL ECONOMIC CONDITIONS: THE OVERALL BUBBLE

Every economy contains artificial indicators. This is why the timing of investment decisions is so difficult and elusive. Real estate, stocks, bonds, and all other markets are difficult to interpret because there is so much information, because timing of cyclical change is never identical from one period to another, and because outside influences affect cyclical movement in different ways. Each of these three factors may create an artificial economic condition in the moment:

1. *Excessive Amounts of Information.* If you try to determine the nature, importance, and timing of the real estate bubble, you will discover a lot of conflicting information. Some real estate experts believe the bubble is about to burst, while others deny its existence. The best you can do with excessive information is to develop perspective about which types of information are valid. If you analyze local real estate based on traditional tests (inventory of properties, spread, and time on the market) and then compare those trends to recent price changes, you can determine whether your local conditions are in a price bubble.

If you search online for any information regarding real estate information, you will discover thousands of sites. These range from academic theories testing how real estate valuation evolves to companies selling products or services, and from organizations acting as dealers between preconstruction buyers and sellers to sites explaining conspiracy theories about real estate. As is true for any other topic, the Internet is a waste heap of information, with only a few gems of valuable (and free) information thrown in with the rest.

The problem with having a lot of information available is determining which sites are worth reading, which ones are only trying to sell you something, and which are simply junk. For a few dollars, anyone can create a professional-looking website and put a lot of information on their page. This alone does not mean it is true, well researched, or worth your time. Just as with stocks, real estate websites come in all shapes and sizes.

2. *Timing of Cyclical Change.* There is no formula for signaling how or when changes in a real estate cycle occur. Every cycle is different and cycles perform differently in each region. At any given moment, a cycle gives off many signs, including false starts in a direction opposite the current trend. Charting

the course of the cycle is easy with hindsight, and the signals can be easily interpreted. These include new construction permits, changes in interest rates, and population/employment shifts. But when you are in the middle of a cycle, you have no idea how emerging signals are going to affect the duration, direction, or strength of a trend.

To cope with the difficulty of chaotic short-term trends, you can only rely on a study of the sources for real supply and demand. These are well known. You are wise to ignore the short-term changes you see in your area, and focus instead on developing trend indicators based on hard data.

3. *The Effect of Outside Influences.* The things that affect real supply and demand—such as employment, building or over-building, and interest rates—affect each region in different ways. You cannot assign weight to any one factor, such as interest rates or overbuilding, because every market is different. Excess construction in one region might have little or no impact on prices, whereas in another region the same degree of construction could bring price trends to a grinding halt.

*   *   *

One fact that makes trend-watching interesting is that you will continually be surprised by what you see. Just as you think you have figured out how markets react to a specific trend, you will witness a repeat of the same circumstances with a completely different market reaction (market means price, speed of sales, etc.). The only thing you cannot expect is consistency.

To demonstrate how varied markets can react, and how they cannot be timed by any formula, you need to study historical bubbles. Chapter 4 explains the causes and outcomes of some famous historical market bubbles.

NOTES

1. www.ubs.com, as of April 13, 2006.
2. John R. Talbot, *Sell Now! The End of the Housing Bubble*

(New York: St. Martin's Press, 2006). Quoted in Dana Perrigan, "A Bull, A Bear, and the Bubble," *San Francisco Chronicle*, March 12, 2006.

3. David Lereah, *Why the Real Estate Boom Will Not Bust* (New York: Doubleday, 2006). Quoted in Dana Perrigan, "A Bull, A Bear, and the Bubble."

4. "Understanding Fannie Mae," at www.fanniemae.com.

5. Federal National Mortgage Association, Government National Mortgage Association, and Federal Home Loan Mortgage Corporation: annual reports.

6. J. N. Tlaga, *How the Fiat Money Is Being Defended*, at www.gold-eagle.com

7. Marc Wilson, "Earthquake Risks Shouldn't Bother Savvy Real Estate Buyers," *San Francisco Apartment Magazine*, March 2006.

CHAPTER 4

How Bubbles Happen

T he history of real estate—and, in fact, of all markets—is a history of emotional overreaction. You see this on both sides of the price swing. When prices are high, investors want to jump onto the investment in the belief that prices will go upward forever. When prices are low, doom and gloom prevails and everyone is frightened out of the market.

These tendencies are described by some as "greed and fear"—two powerful emotions that distort rational thought and destroy investment portfolios. Whether it is greed and fear or just an all too human tendency to react to unexpected events, the outcome is clear. Rather than following the age-old advice to "buy low and sell high," the common pattern is exactly the opposite. People tend to buy high and sell low and, of course, it is very difficult to predict peaks and valleys.

In real estate, one way to recognize the peak of a bubble is when the number of speculators is greater than ever before. Seeing amazing double-digit returns by those already in the market, new people enter and serve as buyers to those who want to

sell. The frenzy accelerates until there are simply no more speculators. The market tops out and then tumbles. But at the peak,
the number of buyers is higher than at any point in the previous
cycle, during which the bubble was expanding.

On the opposite side of the bubble, when prices tumble, they
may fall below the true market value. So a smart market observer
would be able to pick up properties at dirt-cheap prices. This
happens all the time in the stock market, where shares go back
and forth continually; in real estate, it isn't quite as easy.

Real estate bubbles are different than bubbles in stocks or
commodities. The Miami-Dade market is a good example. The
mere excess supply of condo units makes any growth in market
value impossible for at least nine years. In these conditions, why
would anyone want to buy condo units except to live in them?
Once the owner-occupied units have been sold at deep discount,
the rest of the excess supply will simply remain available without
a market.

In the stock market, prices of shares eventually fall far
enough to meet demand, so the market is efficient because it is
auction-based. But corporations are not issuing far more shares
than investors want to buy. In practice, the fact that there exists
only a finite number of shares contributes to each share's value.

In real estate, the bubble-driven creation of more units than
demand requires is an especially troubling trend. You would
think investors would learn from history, and there is plenty of
"bubble history" to observe. But one of the amazing facts about
money and investing is that people simply do not learn. There is
never a shortage of people willing to enter the market at the
wrong time and to invest money foolishly.

This phenomenon is known as the "greater fool theory." This
theory states that a speculator can make money even buying
overpriced products, as long as there is someone else more gull-
ible waiting to pay more.

The greater fool exists and is quite real, but only to a point.
As any pyramid scheme demonstrates, the supply is eventually

exhausted and the "greatest fool" is the last speculator, who ends up overinvested in overpriced and overvalued properties.

The luckiest speculator in the world should be the one who gets out just before the greater fool gets in. That would be true, assuming that the speculator leaves the market once and for all. But in practice, this simply does not happen. When a speculator makes a 30 or 40 percent return on an investment, the tendency is to roll all of that money back in, and to try for an even bigger score. So someone who starts by putting $50,000 at risk on a down payment on one condo and triples that to $150,000 is likely to turn around and try to double or triple that money.

Sometimes, the biggest fool is the person who makes the profit and stays for one transaction too long.

THE PSYCHOLOGY OF EUPHORIA

Everyone has heard about "gold fever." After gold was discovered in California in 1848, thousands of people sold everything and headed for the central California area to make their fortune. They were told that there was so much gold they only had to walk around and pick nuggets up off the ground. And they believed these stories. History reveals, however, that other than some early prospectors, few people made a profit from the California Gold Rush. The primary beneficiaries of the migration were the business owners who provided services to the newly arrived dreamers: those who operated general stores, hotels, saloons, bordellos, and specialty stores selling gold mining equipment.

Even when the truth filtered back east—that prospecting was back-breaking work yielding little if any reward—new people kept arriving. The migration lasted many years beyond the early "easy pickings" days of 1848 to 1849. Something happens to people once they come to believe that they can get rich quickly, whether in a gold rush or in the stock market or in real estate. Euphoria and frenzy replace common sense, and judgment evaporates.

Many people, upon hearing this story and discovering that it

repeats itself over and over, will say, "I would never be that fool-
ish." Even so, you can find many modern examples. The dot-com
and technology craze of the late 1990s, the rush to buy Enron
stock, and of course the many regional real estate bubbles of 2005–
2006 all make this point. Some people do get rich with lucky timing, but *most* recognize the opportunity only after it has passed.

In the early 1980s when gold jumped to $800 per ounce,
thousands of people began buying coins and bullion in the belief
that their money would double or triple in no time. That particular aberration lasted only a short time, and eventually gold sank
back down to less than half of its peak value, where it remained
for the next two decades. But at its very height, the fever to buy
gold in any form was at an absolute peak. This is the pattern seen
repeatedly in bubbles.

Efficient Market or Buying Frenzy?

Some investment theories disagree with this assessment entirely.
The well-known *efficient market hypothesis* states that the current prices of any product reflect all of the information known to
the investing public, and all of that information has been factored
into the price. This hypothesis is most often associated with
stock pricing, but it can be applied equally to real estate. However, the theory would imply that price bubbles cannot exist.
Some people believe that well-informed investors (or speculators) causing overpriced conditions are quickly corrected by a
well-informed market.

This theory ignores the very real euphoria that characterizes
investor behavior, which causes the logical judgment of an otherwise rational individual to suspend itself. One counter-theory to
the efficient market hypothesis may have greater application in
real estate, and thus should be kept in mind when analyzing the
nature of real estate bubbles. This theory states that:

> There are some "behavioral" agents variously subject to animal
> spirits, fads and fashions, overconfidence, and related psycho-

logical biases that might lead to momentum trading, trend chasing, and the like.[1]

The authors making this statement also observed, quite accurately, that even rational speculators may know the market is going to collapse but nonetheless decide to "ride the bubble" to generate continuing high returns. The belief among these individuals is that they will be able to leave the market just in time to avoid being invested when the collapse occurs. But this is self-delusional. The nature of bubbles mandates that they burst when no one expects it. No speculator is wise enough to time his decision perfectly, and it is a human tendency to ignore this very human flaw.

How Speculators Think

Speculators tend to think their starting point is zero (out of 1 to 100) when it might actually be 50 or even 90. The "ideal" situation, of course, is expressed in the idea that speculators want to "stay in the market until the subjectivity probability that the bubble will burst in the next trading round is sufficiently high." But this is not quite as easy as it sounds. When trying to decide exactly when to take their profits, speculators suffer from a blind spot. They "do not know whether they have learnt this information early or late relative to other[s]."[2]

To understand bubbles, you need to understand speculators and how they think. The tendency among speculators is to believe that they are smart enough to recognize the signs that a bubble is about to collapse, sell off their holdings just in time, and move on to other profitable bubble situations while the less informed "greater fool" ends up with overvalued property.

Virtually every real estate speculator believes this.

Another trait of speculators is to believe that everyone knows what they know. If it makes sense to invest in property whose value is growing in double digits, everyone must surely know this. The tendency is to associate with people who agree with one's point of view, to confirm a belief system, and to bolster it.

But this type of mutual knowledge or mutual belief is *not* the same as universal knowledge or belief. So speculators will purchase an overvalued asset in the full knowledge that it is overvalued *and* that, in fact, they might be unable to find a buyer. Even so, the bubble continues to move forward in spite of the logical and obvious fact that it will eventually burst.

"The Tragedy of the Commons"

One attribute of speculation and bubbles in general is that they are often correctible by their own participants. In an "ideal" world, that is, speculators would recognize the destructive outcome of ever-growing prices and would work together to slow down the rate of growth collusion. This would not only serve the larger market, but self-interest as well. But this never happens, because speculation operates on a model similar to that called the "tragedy of the commons."

In this model, several individuals share a common area where cattle graze. This commons is available without restriction to all of the individuals, but it will remain useful as a resource only if it is not overgrazed. When each individual allows only one cow or horse to graze, the system works. But the *tendency* is for the individuals to exploit the lack of restriction and place as many heads of cattle on the commons as possible. As a result, the resource is utterly destroyed.[3]

This model reveals all that you need to know about speculation and bubbles. Yes, it is possible, at least in theory, for participants in a real estate bubble to slow down excessive price growth and to bring order to the market. This assumes that the forces of competition are made subordinate to the force of self-interest.

FAMOUS BUBBLES IN HISTORY

The model for the most excessive bubble possible dates back a few hundred years, to Holland. The "tulipmania" phase was mind-boggling in its excess, but the experience has been repeated many times in other markets, including real estate.

The Dutch Tulip Bubble

By the middle of the seventeenth century, tulip bulbs found a willing market in Holland. Many varieties of tulips are exceptionally beautiful, and the desire among a cross-section of people to own them became extreme:

> The rage for possessing them soon caught the middle classes of society, and merchants and shopkeepers, even of moderate means, began to vie with each other in the rarity of these flowers and the preposterous prices they paid for them. A trader at Harlaem was known to pay one-half of his fortune for a single root, not with the design of selling it again at a profit, but to keep in his own conservatory for the admiration of his acquaintance.[4]

A real bubble ensued, and among its symptoms was the fact that all levels of society became involved in speculation in tulip bulbs. By 1635, prices had risen to ridiculous levels. At that time, 5,000 florins would be more than enough to buy a new carriage, two horses, and a harness set. In comparison, it was not uncommon for people to pay the same amount for a single tulip. The *Semper Augustus* variety was called a "bargain" at 5,500 florins, for example (about $40,000).

Eventually, trading in tulip bulbs reached such high volume that a market was established on the Amsterdam Stock exchange with branches in other cities as well. Of course, during this "craze phase" many people became instantly wealthy, at least in the moment. The craze eventually fizzled out and when it did, early in 1637—meaning the market demand simply evaporated—values of tulip bulbs tumbled. Many wealthy people who had believed they would never again see poverty were ruined overnight.

The South Sea Bubble

Another example was the South Sea Bubble, which covered a period from 1711 to 1715 in England. The South Sea Company was established by Robert Harley, Earl of Oxford. In exchange for taking over £10 million of government debt, the company was granted a monopoly for trade with Spanish colonial interests in South America. Shares were in great demand, and their value rose quickly, although investors had not been told the whole story. For example, it proved impossible to make profits in the venture because King Philip V of Spain only allowed a single cargo of merchandise to travel to South America per year. The venture deteriorated into the slave trade and lost many ships to pirates.

During this era, speculative bubbles became quite common. The debacle of the South Sea Company led to one company's issue of "South Sea playing cards," which contained vivid art-work and poetry about various bubble companies. For example, Puckle's Machine Company marketed a machine claimed to dis-charge both round and square bullets, which was promoted as a device to revolutionize the art of war. Of course, there proved to be enough speculators to drive up the price of shares before the venture crashed. One card in a South Sea playing cards deck, the eight of spades, on the topic of Puckle's machine, read:

> A rare invention to destroy the crowd
> Of fools at home instead of fools abroad.
> Fear not, my friends, this terrible machine,
> They're only wounded who have shares therein.[5]

So shocked were the ordinary investors when South Sea stock tumbled a few short years after formation of the company that one member of Parliament, Lord Molesworth, recommended the heads of the company should be tied inside sacks and thrown into the Thames (in a fashion similar to punishment in ancient Rome in which some offenders were sewn into sacks and tossed into the Tiber). More moderate opinions prevailed, however, and it was decided (in the interest of restoring public confidence) that the government should in effect bail out the South Sea Com-pany. Thus, nine million shares were acquired by the Bank of

England, and the proceeds were used to pay creditors. At the same time, company directors and its cashier were forbidden to leave England for one year while their financial conditions were audited.

Ultimately, all of the company's directors were convicted and ordered to refund their profits; some were jailed in the Tower of London. Overall, more than £2 million was confiscated from the estates of the directors.

The Mississippi Bubble

Another infamous bubble, the Mississippi Scheme, occurred early in the eighteenth century. It was so named because it was a scheme to finance France's plans to colonize the Mississippi valley.

John Law, then director of France's royal bank, bought stock from a French merchant, Antoine Crozat, who held a monopoly on Louisiana commerce. Law formed a new concern called the Mississippi Company and, based on wild promises of profits, was able to sell shares in the new company to speculators. Among Law's hype were his claims that Louisiana was a land rich in gold and silver, and that the Arkansas River contained a large emerald rock. (Expeditions were actually launched specifically to find this emerald.) Stock prices were run up so high and so quickly that the inevitable bubble did burst. The scheme had begun in 1717, but in October 1720 stock values tumbled, followed by a French economic crisis.

U.S. Canals Bubble

The United States has seen its share of famous economic bubbles. The Great Stock Market Crash of 1929 is the best known, but a century earlier, a major industrial bubble involving canals (and railroads) dominated the financial landscape.

At the beginning of the nineteenth century, the United States was a relatively poor country. It did not have a single currency and no national currency controls or other economic policies. The country was still recovering from the expenses of the Revolutionary War only a generation before, and the War of 1812 nearly ruined the country both economically and politically. The Civil War did even greater economic damage, much of which lasted for decades. Most notable among the dramatic changes was the decline of the agrarian economy of the South, and its replacement with manufacturing. By 1885, the United States had become the leading manufacturer in the world, producing one-third of *all* goods sold worldwide. Several important factors influenced the changes between 1800 and 1885, including:

• A huge increase in the U.S. population, which grew from 5.3 million people in 1800 to over 55 million by 1885.

• The discovery of gold in California in 1848. Before this discovery, in 1847, the United States had produced only 47,000 fine troy ounces of gold. By 1856, that number had risen to 2,661,000 troy ounces.

• The U.S. domination of the world cotton industry. The development by Eli Whitney of the cotton gin in 1793 revolutionized the agricultural south for the following century. Between 1800 and 1860, the United States produced five-sixths of the world supply of cotton, making the industry as significant in its day as oil is today.

During the nineteenth century, the United States also developed a steel industry, based on the need to develop a national railroad system (tied to the discovery of gold in California, among other reasons). At the same time, the United States began constructing canals, which ultimately led to a real estate bubble in Chicago.

In the 1820s and 1830s, the major project was the Erie Canal. This project, when completed, lowered travel time between New York and the industrial areas of the country (Detroit and Cleveland) by 10 percent. A second canal, the Welland, expanded Great

Lakes industry to the east by water for the first time. The value of more efficient movement of goods to market led to issuance of canal bonds, which at the time were highly favored as safe investments. As with most speculative activities, people thought there was no way the canal boom could ever lead to a loss.

Also during this period, railroads were moving westward at a rapid pace. In 1820, the country had only a few hundred miles of track. By 1880, more than 120,000 miles were in use, with new rail growth taking place at the rate of 13,000 track miles per year.

The combined investment in infrastructure defined the nineteenth century, but not without some setbacks. Until the 1830s, Chicago real estate was cheaper than East Coast real estate because there was no economic incentive for people to buy property there. But that changed very quickly.

A plan was announced early in the decade for construction of the Illinois-Michigan canal, intended to connect Chicago harbor to Lake Michigan. This canal would form a water connection via the Mississippi River all the way to St. Louis. As a result of this planned canal, real estate prices soared by 1836. The following year, a massive stock price collapse delayed the project, and Chicago's real estate values fell 90 percent. From 1837 through 1842, the entire state of Illinois suffered a depression and ended up in default (along with eight other states). Falling well short of its fast completion schedule, the canal finally required more than ten years to finish. Chicago eventually recovered, but in the period from 1830 to 1840, thousands lost all they had as a consequence of investing in Chicago real estate.

* * *

Lessons can be learned from all of these infamous crashes, of course, as well as from those in more modern times. These include the dot-com and technology crashes of the late 1990s, as well as many stock and real estate crashes overseas. But history reveals several profound lessons about bubbles and crashes, including the fact that memories are short. There are invariably plenty of investors and speculators to ensure funding of the next crash, and this fact will continue to affect real estate and other economic cycles into the future.

THE FIVE PHASES OF EVERY BUBBLE

In the classic model of a bubble, you will see a series of steps that occur over and over, and in all markets. Whether the euphoria occurs in trading of stocks or real estate, the pattern is predictable. There are five distinct phases to every bubble. These are:

- *Phase 1: Economic conditions improve over the past.* Bubbles have beginnings, just as they have endings. And bubbles don't grow spontaneously, but are reactions to the larger economic cycle. Economic policies, such as tax cuts and reduction in interest rates, spark the economy. Indicators such as productivity and employment improve, adding to the general sense of prosperity. This widely acknowledged beginning of an economic cycle invariably accompanies the beginning of real estate and other market cyclical change as well.

Experienced investors understand the cyclical nature of real estate. However, less experienced investors, first-time speculators, and those who leverage heavily to become players tend to believe—wrongly—that any strong price movement trend is going to last forever. Even if this belief is not verbalized, it guides the actions of inexperienced investors and speculators. The belief that a "new economy" is going to cause unending growth and higher prices is irrational. But it has been seen time and again, and it explains why so many people are willing to overpay for real estate in times of strong growth, and happily exceed market value in the belief that only prosperity and more prosperity lie ahead. It may sound like a generalization, but it is true: This *always* happens, and those operating on this belief are *always* wrong.

- *Phase 2: Overinvestment starts and grows.* Economists like to talk about "recovery" as if the previous economic condition were a disease. In this recovery cycle, one important symptom is that, even this early on, overinvestment begins. In the case of real estate, this is often the effect of lower interest rate trends begun in the first phase as part of the improved economic conditions. Lower interest rates and liberalized monetary policies are viewed as sparks to the economy, even though one consequence is the expansion of debt in the form of mortgage lending.

Also during this phase you are likely to witness strong price support caused by the irrational exuberance of speculators. This is accompanied by hyperbolic news stories that encourage further speculation but reveal absolutely nothing about the actual value of real estate. As a consequence, the reporting of real estate trends has an inordinate impact on the market that is well out of proportion to its content. Ironically, you see the same phenomenon when the bubble is under threat of bursting.

On the way up in the price cycle, many stories appear in the press about price growth and liberal financing terms. This encourages people to "get into the market before it's too late." As the bubble continues, more troubling signs foretell negative interest rate news, slow-downs in new construction, and rising foreclosure rates. But because reporting is usually an oversimplification of the facts, it is unreliable as a source for making buy-or-sell decisions. Even so, the press is often the sole or primary source of information for large numbers of speculators.

- *Phase 3: Credit is curtailed near the top.* The irony of the bubble cycle involves interest rate policy as a primary culprit. As rates are lowered to generate healthy economic growth, more and more people qualify for first-time mortgages. This expands the real demand for housing. But in reaction, developers and builders, along with speculators in the market, also tend to meet that real demand with an excess supply. The value of *all* real estate is bolstered by ever-increasing speculation, further encouraged by the accompanying growth in real demand. If lower interest rates were removed from the equation, there would be little speculative incentive (thus, bubbles) and the market would tend to operate efficiently with balanced supply and demand.

As the bubble intensity grows, it is aggravated by a reversal in interest rates. Foreclosures grow because of two factors:

1. Increased payments in interest-only and variable-rate mortgages make once-affordable homes less so.

2. Increased speculation, which sometimes does not pan out, further aggravates the profitability of real estate, even in rising markets.

But is the problem caused by interest rates inching higher? The continuum of real estate bubbles and economic policy is too complex for a simple explanation to provide all of the answers. In questions about prices and inflation, the root causes are never simple. One humorous observation about the complexity of these matters states, "Steel prices cause inflation like wet sidewalks cause rain."[6]

   • *Phase 4: At the top of the bubble, individuals recognize that the bubble exists, but speculation continues.* At the very top of the bubble, the enthusiasm of speculators is infectious. More and more people jump on board (as in the Gold Rush, when prices of covered wagons rose because so many people wanted urgently to get to California and start getting rich). Obviously, speculators in the preconstruction condo market in Florida must have known that a nine-year supply was on the market by 2006 and that prices were amazingly high, even with the contradiction so apparent. Even so, the tendency is to continue to speculate even when the bubble is known to exist.

A good degree of denial is at play during this phase. If you believe that a bubble bursts only when selling pressure exceeds the number of "greater fools," this also implies that knowledgeable real estate speculators (as well as brokers, developers, and lenders) are not actually even aware of changes in selling pressure. This suggestion is difficult to accept, since experts in the field certainly know how to read the signs.

Bubbles may reflect an economic change rather than simple speculative demand. For example, with the purchasing power of the dollar having declined to about one-half its value over the twenty years from 1984 to 2004, you would expect housing prices to double, just to remain relatively the same, given a weaker dollar. Based on a beginning value of "1.00" for 1984, the Bureau of Labor Statistics[7] reports the following value of one dollar at the end of each year:

Year	Value of $1.00	Year	Value of $1.00	Year	Value of $1.00
1984	$1.00	1991	.73	1998	.61
1985	.93	1992	.71	1999	.60
1986	.91	1993	.69	2000	.58
1987	.88	1994	.68	2001	.57
1988	.85	1995	.65	2002	.56
1989	.81	1996	.64	2003	.54
1990	.77	1997	.62	2004	.53

The decline in purchasing power makes any comparison between housing costs and income unreliable. Since a 1984 dollar was worth only 53 cents by 2004, this meant that a family needed nearly twice as many dollars to buy the same goods and services. The purchasing power decline reflects the inverse of increased prices (i.e., inflation), of course, but the study attempted to make the point that this did not matter. Incomes rose to match prices. However, the loss of purchasing power is part of the equation as well. If the 2004 dollar was worth a 1984 dollar, then it would be valid to compare housing costs as a percentage of a family's income. In that case, it would be true that there was no such thing as an economic or real estate bubble.

The combination of speculators unaware of selling pressure and people in denial that bubbles even exist are symptoms that the market is at or near the top of the bubble. Just as purchasers of gold coins in the early 1980s were convinced that prices would rise forever (meaning $800 per ounce was, to them, a *starting point* in the price of gold), or that people sold everything to be able to go to California in 1848 and pick up gold nuggets and become wealthy, common sense is put aside as the market peaks out.

- *Phase 5: Growth stops, usually very suddenly. Prices fall.* The point just before the collapse of any market is typified by subtle changes in the market. In the condo market, for example, you will see increased efforts at attracting overseas buyers (because the market of domestic speculators has already begun to dry up). One symptom that a price trend has peaked is the tendency of many newcomers and amateurs to enter the market. This is especially true in the stock market, but also applies to real estate. As one author wrote in describing symptoms of a market peak, among other signals, "housewives become active in the stock market."[8] Although this is condescending, of course, it efficiently summarizes the point that market peaks are characterized by an influx of buying activity among first-time speculators.

Why don't people leave the market when this occurs? Because there is a tendency among speculators to believe, falsely, that there is an unspoken "agreement" in the market in general. A speculator may say, "I will sell when everyone else sells," as if this agreement were universally applicable. So even the "greater fool" theory is suspended and replaced by the misguided belief among speculators that they know how other speculators will behave.

This "responsive equilibrium" is to a degree the result of "financial hubris," the arrogance that accompanies a string of market successes. But like most forms of hubris, it comes with a blind spot. Speculators invariably believe that they will sell an instant before the bubble bursts. Even so, the bubble eventually does crash in a specific region and usually involves a specific type of property. When it does, those speculators holding property are shocked to discover that, after all, *they* are the greater fools.

*   *   *

You will see these cyclical phases over and over in every bubble and in every type of market. Some bubbles occur quickly and others (notably in real estate) move more slowly. But the last phase—the bursting of the bubble—always happens very suddenly, and always takes the current property owners by surprise.

IDENTIFYING SPECULATIVE MARKETS

A look back at history often shows that major economic and technological change causes long-term bubbles and, quite likely, affects short-term markets as well. On a very broad social scale, major events have a cause-and-effect long-term outcome. The infamous Black Death that decimated Asia and Europe in the fourteenth century led to massive labor shortages and, eventually, to the Industrial Revolution 400 years later; the necessity of making manufacturing processes more efficient created the outcome.

The era of the discovery voyages from the fifteenth to eighteenth centuries vastly expanded trade as well as the range of commodities. The development of commercial centers resulting from these discoveries and the resulting commerce affected Venice, Genoa, and Florence—and, later, Amsterdam, Antwerp, and London. The "social bubbles" and "cultural bubbles" resulting from newly opened trade routes had profound impact on the world and, of course, on economic growth as well. But today, the countries that led exploration of the New World (Italy, Portugal, Spain, Holland) are no longer economically the strongest in the world.

Bubbles come and go in all cultures and in all industries. In the pre-computer era of mid-twentieth-century America, the modes of business and commerce were quite different from what they are today. People used the telephone and the mail for correspondence, bill-paying, and sales. But development of innovations like the computer and the Internet have created economic bubbles of their own. This trend is by no means new. For example, consider the economic bubble created after Henry Ford began assembly-line production of automobiles. By 1910, over 200 auto manufacturers were in business. Today, there are only three domestic manufacturers and all face economic challenges.

Real Demand vs. Speculation

To understand today's real estate bubbles, you need to also appreciate the distinction between economically driven markets and speculative markets. Just as no one in 1910 knew which auto manufacturers would survive, you cannot appreciate a modern market without also knowing that all trends are temporary. Fads come and go, and speculators follow fads from market to market.

In a "real" market, the levels of growth in prices are explained logically and can even be anticipated based on actual economic factors. If an employer is moving to a new city and creating hundreds of new jobs, those employees will need homes. So an astute observer would understand that current home values are likely to increase. There is an identifiable, *real demand,* and it is a known quantity.

There is a distinction between real demand and artificial demand that grows within the bubble, and is caused by liberal interest rate trends and rampant speculation. Real estate trends have been interesting in the sense that they often contradict stock market trends. For example, in the late 1940s after World War II, the stock market averages remained well below pre-1929 levels. Investors feared a second depression and fears about losses in the market kept an entire generation dubious about buying stocks. In comparison, real estate began a long-term boom period as ex-soldiers married and started families.

The famous baby boom, from 1946 through approximately 1964, led to incredible growth rates in real estate. William Levitt became well known in the industry for his large-scale housing developments, Levittown (originally named Island Trees). The site eventually covered 5,500 acres in Bucks County, Pennsylvania, and contained 17,311 single-family homes. Levitt "invented" the modern suburb, appealing to city-dwellers' dreams of escaping cramped urban living conditions and raising a family "outside of the city." The new trend capitalized on the postwar demand for housing and served as a model that has continued ever since.[9]

So a market that begins with real demand and is responded to with real supply (meaning, of course, a reasonable give-and-take between the two sides) may continue for some time. But eventually, the model of the "tragedy of the commons" wins out. Speculators enter the market and create "false demand," or developers accelerate their activity in response to rising prices, finally creating an oversupply—or, to make the offsetting comparison, a "false supply." In the extreme real estate bubble, speculators and developers work together and create their own cross-marketing supply and demand. Only when the supply of new speculators (greater fools) runs out does the whole plan fail.

If you consider the "demand bubble" created by postwar family creation, you can better understand the more avidly observed "supply bubble" in areas like Miami-Dade, Florida. All bubbles are first created by actual market forces, and for sensible reasons. They merely go too far. In this respect, the excess itself is a natural part of the traditional real estate cycle. For example, in postwar America, rapid expansion of the new American suburb led to massive building in satellite communities around many communities. A consequence of this "overbuilding" depressed prices until the next round. This is a typical response to sudden, higher demand. But in the case of the modern bubble, two forces are at work: liberal credit within a virtually unlimited secondary market, and area-specific speculation.

The Real Estate Boom

Throughout the 1950s, real estate prices boomed due to the continuing postwar baby boom demand. But it was real demand and not a bubble. That demand came from people who intended to live in the homes they were buying, and not from speculators. These first-time homebuyers were not considering the investment value of property as a short-term speculative device. Everyone wanted to own a home. It came to be called the American Dream because the entire generation starting families in the 1950s believed that homeownership represented security and success. The many immigrants who arrived in the United States in the 1950s also believed in the American Dream. Homeownership was the epitome of the "success story," and real estate took on an almost sacred importance for both native-born and immigrant families.

These homebuyers may be thought of as "end users" and may be contrasted with speculators. A similar contrast can be made among stamp collectors and dealers seeking profits. Old-fashioned stamp collectors, whose primary interest was collecting, bought and traded stamps from an appreciation of the design art and variation of the product. In contrast, stamp collectors who invested in a rare issue primarily to make a profit experienced none of the aesthetic joy of collecting. By the same argument, real estate speculators view housing as "product" and not as housing.

Real estate buyers of the 1950s also understood that buying a home was only the first phase of the American Dream. From that point forward, a focus became paying off the mortgage. Expectation of profit was low because none of these families intended to ever move. They wanted to pay off the mortgage and own their homes free and clear. Immigrants also adopted the position that by the time of their retirement, the family home should be debt-free.

The European immigrants, especially, held low regard for those who passed debts on to their children, and a cultural requirement among their children was to honor the debts of deceased parents. So in contrast with the modern tendency to treat bankruptcy as a strategy, European immigrants and children of immigrants were likely to consider bankruptcy the ultimate (and permanent) sign of failure.

More Debt Means More Risk

Today's real estate investor has a much different perspective on debt. Many homes are purchased with nothing down, and using interest-only or negative amortization mortgages. This phenomenon adds to the bubble risk in real estate: When homeowners have no real financial stake in properties, increased interest rates naturally lead to increased foreclosure rates.

The overall risk to the American economy rests with what happens post-bubble. The point has been made in earlier chapters that real estate is always local, that bubbles are unique to specific areas, and that there is no logical reason that *all* real estate values have to fall because a bubble bursts in one of these markets. This describes a likely scenario. However, if you combine a reversal in real estate trends with outside events, a different scenario is also possible.

For example, a sudden jump in interest rates will cause widespread defaults and foreclosures among variable-rate borrowers. If, at the same time, unemployment also rises, stock prices fall, and outside events beyond the economy (such as a major domestic terrorist event, for example) combine to create a serious recession.

When you look at the real estate market by itself, the "universal burst" of a bubble is unlikely. But history has shown that the combination of events often leads to larger economic disasters. The 1929 crash of the stock market did not cause a worldwide depression, but there were worldwide economic problems during the 1930s. The crash was only a symptom of a market bubble crash caused by many events. But at the same time, the worldwide depression was also caused by complex matters beyond the stock market. For example, the reparations required of Germany to be paid to the allies after World War I led to the currency collapse in Germany and, as a consequence, throughout Europe as well. Similarly, stock market and commodities bubbles in Japan, Texas, and elsewhere all led to massive "boom and bust" cycles.

So localized bubbles come and go without widespread or long-term effect on the rest of the economy. But outside events can also cause much greater damage than the cyclical downward spiral in real estate after a period of strong growth.

Chapter 5 takes this concept forward to explain how you can recognize the signs that a bubble is about to burst.

NOTES

1. Dilip Abreu and Marjus K. Brunnermeier, "Bubbles and Crashes," *Econometrica*, January 2003.

2. Ibid.

3. Garrett Hardin, "The Tragedy of the Commons," *Science Magazine*, December 1968 (based on a parable published by William Forster Lloyd in 1833).

4. Charles Mackay, *Extraordinary Popular Delusions and the Madness of Crowds*, 2nd edition (London: Office of the National Illustrated Library, 1852).

5. Ibid.

6. Roger Blough (Chairman, U.S. Steel), in *Forbes*, August 1, 1967.

7. U.S. Bureau of Labor Statistics, at www.bls.gov.

8. Marc Faber, *Tomorrow's Gold* (Hong Kong: CLSA Books, 2003).

9. Peter Bacon Hale, "Levittown: Documents of an Ideal American Suburb," Art History Department, University of Illinois at Chicago, at www.uic.edu; and "Building the Suburban Dream," State Museum of Pennsylvania, 2003.

The Four Major Signs
of Coming Change

M arkets tend to act in a predictable manner. The immediate
signals of pending change are difficult to interpret in the
moment, but there are consistent and repetitive signs that things
are changing. One advantage you have in identifying bubbles is
that the fundamental signals are fairly easy to spot.

In the traditional real estate cycle, identifying the current
trends is often subtle. There is nothing subtle about real estate
bubbles, so it makes sense to understand how to recognize the
four major signs that the market is about to change:

1. Development trends
2. Speculation
3. Basic market statistics
4. Lending

These four signs can help you to determine the relative conditions of real estate in your region. Knowing how to read the sig-

nals also helps you to identify the existence of real estate bubbles and to anticipate when they are likely to burst.

LOGICAL ANALYSIS, NOT EMOTIONAL RESPONSE

A lot of literature is devoted to various theories about timing the stock market, taking specific positions, and making profits in any kind of market. But very little exists to explain the same theories regarding real estate. This is due partially to the fact that stocks can be easily traded on a moment's notice, whereas a real estate transaction involves bigger dollar amounts and extends over many weeks, often months. The same essential market facts are at play economically, and real estate reacts to the supply and demand factors of the market just like stocks. Reaction time is not as immediate, and the cost of transactions is far higher than for stocks, but the underlying facts remain unchanged.

Going Against the Crowd

One popular stock market theory says you should act as a contrarian, because the majority is always wrong when it comes to reading signals and to timing investment decisions. This theory is equally useful for real estate as for stocks.

Some people reject contrarian investing on the mistaken belief that the strategy is oversimplified, and that it ignores some realities. Others reject contrarian investing by citing the *efficient market hypothesis*. This hypothesis presumes that all prices are correct because all information about a product (real estate, stocks, etc.) is known to the investing public, so today's price is the right price. This is a comforting theory, but the documented proof of real estate bubbles contradicts it. Additionally, the historical recurrence of stock market panics and speculative bubbles shows that the efficient market theory aside, markets tend to be highly inefficient at certain times, and that irrational behavior cannot be discounted.

The efficient market hypothesis even has been used to "prove" that bubbles cannot exist. In other words, because the market is presumed to be efficient in terms of valuation, as the argument goes, a bubble is not possible. This observation of behavior under the efficient market hypothesis is misleading. It is a misapplication of logic because it is based on a *theory* and not on actual behavior. The behavior of speculators, developers, and investors makes it clear that their view of markets (especially when operating within a bubble) is highly inefficient.

Interpreting Signs Differently

There is a degree of efficiency within the market, of course. Vast numbers of individuals and institutions have been able to invest in highly profitable stocks, for example, when the positive signs were there. This indicates that the contrarian approach does not exclude the possibility of the majority being right some of the time. But it is not stock selection that defines a contrarian—it is the way people read signals. That distinction is a significant one. This confusion has led to a general misunderstanding of contrarian investing.

A limited view assumes that the contrarian simply buys when everyone is selling, and vice versa. But in actual practice, contrarians acknowledge that the majority is right when the signals are obvious. They just do not interpret those signals in the same way as most people. A good example is the ever-popular PE ratio, which compares price to earnings. The higher the PE multiple, the more inflated a stock's price. History has shown that low-PE stocks perform better than high-PE stocks; but those very high-PE stocks continue to be more popular among investors. The contrarian recognizes the flaw in this popular thinking and makes decisions based on some indicators that go opposite the common thinking and belief.

Whether in stocks or real estate, a contrarian recognizes that people often time their decisions based on a misreading of the signals. This is why buying activity tends to accelerate as market value reaches a peak, and it reaches its height just before price trends reverse. It also explains why selling is likely to be at its highest level when prices are the most depressed. The two emotions that usually guide the market are greed and fear, and this explains why people buy and sell at exactly the worst times. They react based on greed and fear, rather than on a sensible, analytical approach. The advice to "buy low and sell high" seems condescendingly obvious, but it is not. It is profoundly important advice, because most people do the opposite: The tendency to buy high and sell low is far more common among investors.

If you apply the contrarian point of view to any market, you realize that an intelligent and logical analysis of the market's conditions will dictate timing, and that emotional reactions invariably mislead you. In the stock market, you see a day-to-day gut reaction to short-term and highly technical trends, and this explains why people lose in the market. In real estate, the same tendencies (based on greed and fear) can be equally damaging to your net worth.

Look at Local Signs

Some market experts have adopted the view that housing acts just like the stock market. Comparing real estate to the stock market is inaccurate for many reasons. Stocks trade rapidly and with little costs, and price is set through an auction marketplace. Real estate trades in a completely different environment. Even the basic supply and demand features of the two markets are entirely dissimilar. And, perhaps most important, regional factors apply only to real estate and not to stock.

In stocks, a specific sector's trends can drag down an entire group of stocks. For example, Merck's problems with lawsuits can depress all pharmaceutical stocks. This is so partly because stocks do not trade regionally; they *are* universal. But real estate is not the same as stock. It is local in nature. So the belief that "current economic conditions, combined with the actions of overly aggressive lenders, leave the housing market ripe for a major crash"[1] is overly broad. It implies that when "the bubble" bursts, it will burst everywhere. And that is simply not true.

The broad advice to get out of real estate altogether should be tempered with the advice to get out of real estate if your local market is in a bubble. Otherwise you should understand that a bubble across the country (or even 100 miles away) will not affect your real estate value.

In doing your logical analysis, therefore, the regional factor cannot be ignored, because it defines the market in every respect. Even in analyzing trends within a specific market, it is important to remember that real estate is always local. This means that any study of bubbles and investor behavior is local as well. Thus, if a specific regional bubble does burst, there are likely to be some residual effects, but a market-wide effect is very unlikely. The conditions of a national market or even broad geographic region (northeast or southwest, for example) are interesting barometers of overall trends, but they are only averages. These statistics do not reveal what is actually going on in your immediate region.

For example, let's assume that a specific region is reporting a large decrease in median housing prices. This is blamed on overbuilding, higher-than-average unemployment, and a long-term demographic trend in which people are leaving the area and migrating elsewhere. This all sounds grim for real estate. However, these are only averages. They do not take into account the specific realities of your city or county. So if your area is experiencing high demand for housing because a major employer has just opened a plant, housing is in short supply, and the local population is growing, these are all positive signs. The local trends are what really count, rather than a regional or national average, because that is what affects the real estate market where you live.

This observation is true in non-bubble real estate environments as well as in bubble situations. Real estate trends are very local, and anyone who has invested in stocks or mutual funds is likely to overlook this. So when you read about national average prices rising or falling, it has nothing to do with valuation in your town. This is the important distinction that is easily overlooked.

So how do you know when a real estate bubble is underway and when it is about to burst? Look for these four major signs that your local market is about to change.

SIGN #1: DEVELOPMENT ACTIVITY STOPS MAKING SENSE

A general assumption is made in the market that experts—those dealing in real estate professionally—understand the cyclical factors better than the average person. Thus, they are better able to time their investment decisions. In practice, however, you will see time and again that these insiders make bad decisions just like everyone else. They may even tend to make worse timing decisions because they are too close to see what is happening.

In the stock market, the scandals of the early 2000s included the revelation that market analysts often gave poor advice to clients. In fact, the problem was so severe that the conflict of interest among insiders was one of the major areas demanding reform. As it turned out, the very market insiders advising clients seemed to be the least able to predict profitability. This is ironic, but not surprising. Analysts, stockbrokers, and financial planners have never been able to outperform the market for their clients, and the belief that these insiders can help anyone to experience better than average returns is a myth. The same observation applies to real estate. No expert can help you to predict future valuation, least of all those with a vested interest within the market itself.

Developers want to encourage a belief in a strong real estate economy because they need buyers for their properties. Speculators need other speculators willing to pay higher prices for properties. Real estate agents (who, far from being experts, are licensed to sell real estate after passing a simple test) are motivated by commission earnings and will *always* tell prospective buyers that the time is right to buy property today. You will rarely hear a salesperson advise you to hold off because prices are too high.

The incentive, then, is for insiders to be out of touch with valuation of the product they deal with on a daily basis. The need for a healthy market (to generate income) clouds judgment. The need for a growing supply of new buyers makes insider advice questionable at best. Developers are not immune from this tendency.

Irrational Behavior

An examination of past bubbles reveals that those with the greatest financial stake in a market tend to act in the most irrational manner, and tend to put ever-higher amounts of money into the market as the bubble grows. The insider ignores signs of change because they tend to seek only those facts supporting their desire for ever-higher profits. People who want to believe in a specific reality tend to seek facts supporting their belief, and to reject facts contradicting the belief. The hubris of the insider has led to the loss of many fortunes. This is why insiders like developers continue to justify their investment even when factors (such as the existence of multiyear housing supplies) defy the decision. It is always possible to develop a rationale even as the collapse of the bubble is imminent. The players tend to justify their behavior, even when it is clearly irrational.

To an outside observer, developer behavior in a bubble environment appears to be irrational, especially in hindsight. Even during the bubble itself, those with the most to gain or lose tend to ignore what is actually happening within the bubble. The general belief—and a misguided one—is that a speculator will simply know when the bubble is at its height, and will be skilled enough to identify the exact point at which to sell. This has been called a "responsive equilibrium," the belief among speculators that other speculators will synchronize their decisions to sell.

In reality, though, these speculators "do not become aware of selling pressure by other rational agents until it crosses this threshold."[2] The threshold is the decision that it is time to get out, and the implication here—supported by historical bubble behavior—is that by the time someone knows it is time to sell, it is already too late. However, it can also be recognized—and with amazing clarity if you know what to look for—as it is going on as well.

Consider the Miami-Dade preconstruction condo market. Even with a nine-year supply of condo units on the market, development showed no signs of slowing down as of early 2006. The demand among speculators funded development, and plenty of speculators were available demanding more and more units to be built, even when the market activity was between existing and new speculators, and absent any *real demand* within the market. From the developer's point of view, as long as there exists a ready demand—thus funding for construction—the activity will continue regardless of real market conditions.

Developers themselves are prone to speculate in this market. When they see speculators making short-term, double-digit returns on preconstruction activity, it encourages them to place themselves in ever-higher risk positions. Why sell to a speculator who is going to double his money in two months? Why not develop more and more units and sell them directly to the next round of speculators?

Spotting the Obvious Signs

You can easily recognize speculative fever of this type by observing two related factors:

1. Development activity
2. Inventory of available properties on the market

When the bubble is nearing its "burst point," the activity among developers will have grown to record-high levels. At the same time, inventory of current homes (or condos) will have grown to unsupportable levels, well beyond a full year. As developers convert their passive activity of supplying properties to speculators and become speculators themselves, it is a sure sign that the bubble cannot sustain itself for much longer.

Recognizing this trend is easy, but there is a tendency within the market to view the situation with unbridled (and unjustified) enthusiasm. You will see growing disdain aimed at bubble theories, replaced by growth in the "greed factor," in which all players in the market (developers, real estate agents, investors, speculators, and first-time homeowners) conclude that everyone else is getting rich and it is time to jump onto the trend, buy up real estate, and reap those short-term, double-digit profits.

In the typical non-bubble real estate cycle, after the uptrend has peaked, development activity slows down and then stops altogether. Excess supply then waits out lagging demand, and the cyclical pattern goes into a downtrend. The greater the oversupply of properties, the longer it takes for real demand to return to the environment. That is the "normal" course of events.

In a bubble economy, the predictable cyclical pattern is turned on its head. Developers do not react to a sudden slowdown in demand; instead, as real demand disappears, their development activity accelerates. Developers (and speculators) most certainly know at this point that the demand is artificial and driven by speculation, but they do not believe that they will be the "greater fool" stuck with overvalued properties.

What Should You Do?

When these conditions exist, you would be wise to stay out of the specific market and avoid the risk of becoming overinvested in inflated properties. Resist the temptation to "get your share" of the gold. Recognize that eventually those speculators with the most to lose will, of course, lose the most.

The greed factor is very compelling. First-time speculators may start out investing in a single unit or house. In three months, they double their money, so selling at that point is a success story. However, it is difficult to take the profits and walk away. The human tendency is to buy two, three, or five properties so that in the next round, they will make even more profits. And it isn't just the initial capital that is put at risk. Many people mortgage their homes and max out their credit cards to put as much as possible into the "sure thing" of rapidly accelerating real estate. Many people have been financially ruined by allowing their objectivity to give way to greed.

Avoiding this market is good advice. A second suggestion is equally sound: If you own property subject to the impending bubble, sell it now and take your money out. For example, if you are living in a condo unit in a city where condo values have risen dramatically in recent years, check the existing inventory of condos in your area. If the current supply has been growing higher and higher, sell now before the bubble bursts. Take your profits and buy a different kind of property in the city; or invest in property where current inventories are much lower and within a rational level (under one year's supply, for example). It may not be enough protection to simply move your capital from one property to another one of the same category. For example, if the bubble is growing in single-family housing, it will not protect you to take profits now if you are going to reinvest them in another single-family property. For example, by mid-2006 Chicago single-family home sales slowed down as the inventory grew to five years. If this proves to be a bubble, anyone who sells their home at the top cannot avoid problems by buying another home in Chicago. An investor may prefer purchasing commercial property or raw land; and a homeowner may want to seek property outside of the affected bubble area. Even if you are not a speculator, your equity can be adversely affected when you own property of the same type that is being overdeveloped today.

SIGN #2: SPECULATION INCREASES NEAR THE PRICE TOP

Speculators are not rational thinkers when bubbles are at their height. A long-standing belief within the market is that "traditional bubbles could not arise in markets characterized by a rational pricing process."[3] However, the truth is far from the misguided assumption that speculators act rationally. And even the idea that asset pricing is based on fundamental value is not necessarily true. The question is far more complex than the simple identification of whether speculative activity is rational or irrational. There is no clear dividing line.

When speculators enter markets, it is usually the result of recognizing an immediate opportunity. It is rational to take advantage of a situation where prices are rising rapidly, and in which demand (real or otherwise) is creating more and more pressure on prices. However, there is also a tendency for speculators to continue turning money over within a speculative venture long after the rationale has passed. This is a gradual process, a "slippery slope" you can see in any market, and one observed over and over in the stock market. In real estate, the same phenomenon is seen the most at the height of a bubble.

Even the wisest and most introspective speculator is likely to lose sight of the *risk* factors involved in short-term real estate, notably in cases where the supply far exceeds the demand. However, this reality seems to escape analysis, as do the sensible valuation models available to everyone.

Believing the Unbelievable

There are two ways to "value" real estate. The analytical (fundamental) approach recognizes that before placing money into real estate, an investor should estimate three determinants:

1. Return on the investment
2. Value of the asset by an assumed sales date

3. A discount rate to be used for defining future returns in terms of current value[4]

The fundamental approach cannot be disputed in terms of its reliability and application to real estate.

The second method of valuation is far more irrational but is more popular during real estate bubbles. Under this second method, a single belief rules: *The price of property today will be replaced by a higher price tomorrow*. This very belief itself is, in fact, the best available definition of a bubble. Fundamentals do not apply and are, in fact, ignored, and the entirely irrational belief that prices will continue to rise indefinitely rules the thought process.

The belief overlooks and even rejects the logical fact that there can be no rational expectation of indefinite increases in price. If speculators were asked directly whether they believe this, they would deny it. However, beliefs aside, speculators do operate as though the unbridled growth in market value were the reality. Most speculators don't believe that bubbles exist, and they certainly don't think they can ever burst.

There are even well-documented efforts in the hottest of markets to ridicule the notion that there could be a real estate bubble. Individuals who organize websites promoting this concept invariably have a financial stake in having its subscribers believe this as well. For example, they may be acting as go-betweens for current speculators and new ones, or between developers and speculators. Clearly, if people became fearful about the safety of their capital, these services would quickly lose their income base.

What to Look For

You can recognize the height of a bubble by the accelerated "pump and dump" taking place in the market. This term is known well in the stock market: It refers to the practice of buying stock and then promoting its value to others, through advertisements, telemarketing, or investment websites. The hope is that other investors will buy shares, driving up the price. When that happens, the original investor sells at an inflated profit. This is illegal under federal law.

These regulations do not extend to real estate speculation, even though the same kinds of questionable promotions occur. The hype and wild promises of unimagined riches you can make in real estate are all aimed at bringing more speculators into an already saturated market.

One sure way to recognize when bubbles are nearing the top is when it becomes difficult to find more speculators. Once capital dries up—which may happen quite suddenly—the whole thing simply collapses just like a pyramid scheme.

The added tendency for current speculators to keep prices up by increasing their stake in inflated properties is a type of desperation. It may begin out of greed, but at some point even the most devoted speculator realizes that the market is about to collapse. This is when they begin offering special "deals" for new speculators, putting more of their own money at risk, and promoting speculation out of the immediate area or even overseas.

Just before the bubble bursts, you also will see higher-than-ever optimism among speculators about potential for greater growth. When the bubble is young, speculators tend to keep things quiet, recognizing that they are in on a good deal. But bubbles always accelerate, requiring greater capital and more people. So the mood of optimism, which is of course artificial and unjustified, becomes the article of faith within the local area. That is a sure sign that things are about to go south, and the time to avoid the market altogether (or, if you are in the market, to sell as quickly as possible).

SIGN #3: MARKET STATISTICS TURN NEGATIVE

A third sign that the market is about to change is found in the fundamentals. These work in all markets. In the stock market, a specific company's operating revenue and profits, its dividend rate and earnings per share, and its position within a sector, all determine *value* and dictate future growth or decline in value. The same is true in real estate, although reading the fundamentals involves different processes.

One factor you will see repeatedly in bubbles is a growing tendency to focus on price and short-term profits. As this occurs, the fundamentals are considered less and less important and are even ignored entirely. In the stock market, rapid growth in a company's price leads to exclusive emphasis on price, even when the fundamentals clearly do not support that price level.

In the real estate market, you can consider the fundamentals to include new permits for development, sales levels and time required to complete a sale, deep discounts developing as expressed in the spread and often changing rapidly, and a growing inventory accompanying higher prices. Because such trends occur locally, you cannot rely on national averages but should seek this information from the local MLS agency, real estate brokers, and lenders.

New Permits

If you monitor the number of permits issued in your city or county, you will be able to identify the development trend in the near future. Permits tend to precede actual construction by several months, so when the number of new permits changes over a period of time, you can anticipate the effect on the current inventory of homes.

In the non-bubble real estate cycle, new permits tend to begin falling off *after* the cycle has peaked. Developers follow the trend and do not stop building until demand has already fallen. But in a bubble, a different effect can be identified to spot when bubbles are approaching the peak. Being able to identify in advance the likelihood of a bubble bursting is clearly an advantage. When prices continue to rise, sales are strong, and you see a large increase in new permits applied for and granted, that is a sign that the bubble is nearing its burst point. Just as stock market investment and volume tend to accelerate as prices approach the top, the same is true in real estate. But developers drive the trend by accelerating the permit application process.

This method is more accurate than the more popular analysis of units under construction. It is true that units being built today will be available on the market in coming months, but this has already been factored into current prices and buying patterns. The permit statistics are less visible and are often ignored by speculators and investors. However, it is quite easy to find local permitting trends with a visit to City Hall.

Sales Statistics

The length of time properties remain on the market is another sign that anticipates changes in demand and, in bubble environments, an impending burst in demand. In a vigorous, healthy market, supply and demand remain closely matched, as seen in a consistent amount of time between listing and sale of properties. However, even as prices continue to rise, an early sign that the bubble is ending may be an increase in the time required to complete a sale.

For example, it may have taken an average of 45 to 60 days during the past year to complete sales. This is a very fast turnaround time. However, in the last three months, you see that the time on the market is beginning to slip upward; last month the average was between 60 and 75 days, for example. This can occur even when prices are still rising, but it foreshadows a more important overall trend: the gradual decline in demand.

This decline does not occur because there are fewer buyers. It may occur because, in the highly profitable bubble environment, an oversupply of units is on the market or being built. The demand remains steady and price support may come from current speculators selling to new speculators. This explains why the time on the market is growing, and is likely to get worse. The price growth is artificial, and this disparity (between time on the market and price) is a red flag telling you that the bubble is coming to an end, and soon.

A related trend is the number of units sold each month. This can be a confusing statistic because when sales begin to fall some speculators will explain that this means prices will be driven even higher. Looking at only one side of the equation—in this case a dwindling supply—is dangerous, because it assumes that the other side—demand—is continuing to grow. In reality, the reduction in units sold may reflect a reduction in demand. It also is one of the signs that prices are being driven high by exchanges between speculators, while real demand is far below current sales levels.

When you see the number of units sold per month declining—especially as prices continue to rise—that is a sign that the price trend is artificial and the bubble is likely to burst soon. The fact that current speculators tend to ignore this is only one more attribute of the "speculation fever" you see at the top of all bubbles.

Deep Discounts in Sales Prices

The spread is also a reliable indicator, and it is useful in all types of markets. In a non-bubble real estate cycle, a widening discount between asked and sold prices indicates softening demand. Of course, as the spread narrows, it also implies that demand is growing.

In a bubble real estate economy, the same rules apply. But at the very top of the bubble, you are likely to see growing discounts, which may develop rapidly. This occurs because real demand cannot match new construction, so speculators need to find new money to come into the market. They need to find the "greater fool" to take properties off of their hands. To do so, they need to give up a portion of their profits, so listed properties are sold below asked price.

This version of the spread exists in the artificial bubble and not as part of the traditional real estate cycle. One way to tell the two apart is by the speed with which the exceptionally high spread develops. At or near the price top, all current speculators realize—suddenly—that their holdings are overpriced, and they begin offering discounts to get out quickly.

Growing Inventory/Growing Prices

The phenomenon of real estate bubbles is a study in contradiction. Prices rise while the inventory of units on the market also rises. You would expect excess inventory to drive prices downward. That would occur if the market consisted entirely of real demand. But when speculators enter the bubble and drive prices upward, the tendency is for developers to overbuild in response. As long as there are more speculators available, developers will build units. They will respond to any type of demand as long as the check clears.

This is why the most common symptom of a real estate bubble is the oddity of excess supply (often in the extreme) accompanied by ever-higher prices. The speculator-driven bubble placed artificial demand for more units on developers. When speculators invested minimal capital and leveraged their preconstruction purchases, lenders carried the difference and, in many cases, developers funded the difference as well. So even as speculators parlayed their capital into a larger number of units, actual risk was spread among other speculators, developers, and lenders.

This trend—excess supply accompanied by rising prices— defies the classic economic theories about supply and demand. It is easy to spot and identify. And it is, perhaps, the most obvious of all signs that a bubble is nearing its end.

SIGN #4: LENDING STATISTICS BECOME OMINOUS

One of the realities that contributes to bubbles and, in fact, supports and may even cause them, is the use of liberal monetary policies by lenders. As previously demonstrated, the federally created secondary market for mortgage debt has created a very leveraged investment forum in which investors finance mortgages. This is accomplished through the marketing of mortgage pool shares. The organizations in this secondary market (GNMA, FNMA, and FHLMC) have very little equity value, with debt holdings and loan guarantees ranging between 70 and 120 times total equity.[5]

For the local conventional lender, the existence of the secondary markets encourages virtually unlimited lending practices. The homeowner makes a loan application with the local lender or through one of the dozens of mortgage companies such as Countrywide, Ditech, and others. The company granting the loan sells that loan to the secondary market, where the loan is pooled and shares sold off. As long as there are willing investors seeking interest on secured debt, there is essentially an unlimited supply of money available to lend.

This situation creates "risk-neutral" lenders. Because they act as conduits for the secondary market and do not place their own reserves at risk, it also means that the market matches an unlimited source of lending with a potentially unlimited supply of investors. Lenders, for this reason, tend to focus on *compliance* with secondary market rules and the meeting of income requirements; and they pay virtually no attention to whether a particular property represents a safe or a risky asset. The evaluation of a particular loan is not based on the size (risk exposure) of the loan, but on ensuring that the borrower is qualified. Neither does the loan process evaluate a property and its potential for return on investment. As a result, lenders tend to test qualification for a loan, but have no mechanism for determining whether the property itself is a "good risk." The person approving loan applications is not the person bearing the risk.

Bubbles are created by this interplay not only because funds are unlimited, but because borrowers bear little or no risk in the market offering unlimited debt financing. Thus, a borrower is more attracted to high-risk real estate (in other words, cheaper "bargain" properties, which also represent greater investment risks). And this makes sense because the borrower does not lose in the highly leveraged owner-occupied market (where zero down payment is common). The lender bears all of the risks.

The outcome here demonstrates how bubbles are created: Because borrowers invest in and drive up the market value of higher-risk real estate, the value of these properties moves higher than its true (fundamental) value.

When does this situation eventually turn ominous and how can you recognize when this happens?

Defaults and Foreclosures Increase

Lending policies and the unlimited supply of money actually may create and worsen the bubble itself. As the situation continues, those higher-risk properties will affect the default and foreclosure rates for lenders. It is more likely that the higher-risk properties are going to be defined as highly leveraged (little or no down payment) and existing in "depressed" areas (you will find fewer high-risk, lower-yielding properties in neighborhoods where property values exceed the average for the region).

So speculative activity (such as the preconstruction market) or highly leveraged home buying both contribute to bubbles and may also provide their defining characteristics. In the midst of "bubble enthusiasm," speculators and homeowners see only the amazing and seemingly unending double-digit growth in property values. They tend to ignore the creeping trend in defaults and foreclosures.

A *default* means that the borrower has fallen behind in payments and the lender has issued notification that the loan has been placed in default status. When this occurs, homeowners may get the wake-up call and find some way to get payments caught up—borrowing from a family member, selling other property, or cashing in savings, for example. Those that do not find their properties going into *foreclosure*. A default can be cured by catching up payments plus penalties. But once a property goes into foreclosure, it is unlikely that the original homeowner will be able to retain ownership. Once payments have fallen behind, lenders will want to sell and recover their money as quickly as possible.

One sign that the bubble is getting close to bursting (or at least slowing down) is an increase in local default and foreclosure rates. Only about 3 percent of homes are foreclosed nationally, so you are not likely to see a big jump in the percentage of foreclosures in a short period of time. However, the percentage of loans in default may be far higher than actual foreclosure rates; so as you see an increase in default levels, that may be a better indicator of a bubble's status.

For example, as of the fourth quarter of 2005, the following states reported the highest past-due (default) rates in the nation[6]:

State	Past Due	In Foreclosure	Foreclosures as % of Defaults
Alabama	8.0%	0.9%	11.3%
Georgia	6.9	1.2	17.4
Indiana	7.4	2.8	37.8
Ohio	6.7	3.2	47.8
Tennessee	6.9	1.2	17.4
Texas	7.8	1.1	14.1
West Virginia	6.8	1.2	17.6

Note: Not included on this list are Louisiana and Mississippi, whose results were distorted due to losses in the 2005 hurricane reason, especially from Katrina.

Although actual foreclosure rates do not necessarily follow the trend, the trends in Indiana and Ohio are vastly more alarming than the other five states because the proportion of defaulted loans ending up in foreclosure is so much greater than the average. So in evaluating the meaning of this trend, look for an increase in foreclosure rates in relation to defaults, rather than watching only one or the other. If the foreclosure rate increases relative to defaults, it is a danger signal indicating that the bubble is coming to an end. As with all trends, it is the movement and change over time that is most revealing, and not just the latest numbers.

The default and foreclosure trend serves as a type of lender report. The greater these negative outcomes, the greater the likelihood that "real equity" in properties is far less than indicated current "market value," meaning that market value has been exaggerated by the bubble.

Adjustable-Rate Mortgages

One characteristic of bubbles is the tendency for an increased number of adjustable-rate loans (ARMs), enabling more and more people to qualify for loans (based on secondary rate qualification). But when rates rise, the problems begin. Defaults are likely to follow because some people will no longer be able to afford higher payments.

Some national factors also serve as warning signs affecting lender activity and reporting. Most obvious among these, of course, are higher interest rates and loan costs. The higher the costs, the fewer people will qualify for loans. This means that a growing number of new borrowers cannot be sustained forever. When rates rise, so do ARM payments.

By definition, a bubble cannot be sustained indefinitely, if only because all demand is finite. Whether speculators or first-time homebuyers, there is a limited number of people who will serve as end users. Some websites promoting real estate investment make arguments that cannot be supported. For example, "It is all right to finance with an adjustable-rate mortgage because property values are rising in double digits" is an inaccurate point of view that may easily lead to the wrong conclusions. Those property values are rising due to the bubble and not to real demand. Therefore, for those homeowners who end up overpaying for real estate using adjustable-rate mortgages are taking the extra risk that when markets turn downward, they will be doubly penalized: by lower values *and* higher rates. Under this scenario, the rate of defaults and foreclosures inevitably grows.

WHAT ABOUT THE BOOMERS?

There are those who say that all the trend watching and identifying signs of change is completely unnecessary. Their argument goes, "Baby boomers are about to retire, so real estate demand will keep growing no matter what happens."

This theory ignores an important reality: Most baby boomers already own property and will not be a source of greater demand upon retirement. In fact, if any significant changes occur as baby boomers retire, it is more likely to be *less* demand for single-family homes. Upon retirement, baby boomers are likely to seek smaller homes, condos, or retirement community living. So the traditional three-bedroom suburban home may end up over-supplying a shrinking market in the near future.

Chapter 6 shows how different types of properties are affected by bubbles.

NOTES

1. John R. Talbot, *The Coming Crash in the Housing Market* (New York: McGraw-Hill, 2003).

2. Dilip Abreu and Markus K. Brunnermeier, "Bubbles and Crashes," *Econometrica*, January 2003.

3. Marie-Christine Adam and Ariane Szafarz, "Speculative Bubbles and Financial Markets," *Oxford Economic Papers*, October 1992.

4. Joseph E. Stiglitz, "Symposium on Bubbles," *Journal of Economic Perspectives*, Spring 1990.

5. Federal National Mortgage Association, Government National Mortgage Association, and Federal Home Loan Mortgage Corporation: annual and quarterly reports.

6. Mortgage Bankers Association, end of fourth quarter, 2005.

Bubbles by Property Type

Most people involved with real estate limit their interests to residential property. This occurs through home ownership as well as through investing. People who speculate in property or buy investments as fixer-uppers, flips, or long-term rentals invariably start out in the residential market. However, it is also possible to experience real estate bubbles in other types of property. This chapter explains the methods of valuation for the major types of property and explores the sources of bubbles by type of property.

FIVE UNIVERSAL TRUTHS EVERYONE NEEDS TO KNOW

As a starting point, consider the fact that some universal truths apply to all kinds of real estate and all kinds of investments. These truths dictate the economic supply-and-demand attributes of property. They include the following five points:

1. *Value does not increase spontaneously or for no reason.* There is a lot of "magic thinking" in the world. (Magic think-

ing describes people's superstitions and irrational beliefs. A gambler's "lucky shirt" is an example.) Children may believe that by wishing something to happen, they can make it occur. Adults usually abandon these beliefs, but may continue to operate on the principles of magic thinking, especially when it comes to investing.

One example is the widespread belief that when a person invests money, the value paid is the starting point. In other words, value will rise from that point forward. But investors actually have no way of knowing whether investment values will rise or fall if they don't know *when* they have entered the cycle. Each person's investment value will differ according to when they entered the cycle. At some point during a bubble, the actual price of property will exceed its fundamental value, and someone investing without thorough analysis has no way of knowing where that point is.

The tendency to believe that value simply grows, without examining the root causes, is a dangerous one and can mislead you into making bad decisions. Whether property values rise due to real demand or as the result of speculative fever (a bubble), it is imperative that you identify the underlying causes. If you conclude that real demand is, indeed, the major factor causing real estate prices to rise and you believe this will continue into the future, your conclusions would be much different than if you can find no real demand whatsoever. And remember, *greed* is the controlling emotion as prices rise (just as *fear* dominates on the way down). People become blinded to the facts when they see easy profits in their future, and this emotion leads to the irrational belief that real estate is a "sure thing."

2. *The real estate market is not the same as the stock market.* It is easy to assume that all markets operate on more or less the same principles. This is simply not so. The stock market is highly liquid and transactions are executed quickly and for little cost. Stocks are bought and sold at auction. Stock is usually

paid for in cash for the most part; a limited margin activity is not commonplace for most individuals or even for most institutional investors. And stock itself has no tangible value, but represents a partial ownership in a corporation (the corporation, in turn, owns the tangible assets).

Real estate is very illiquid and transactions are both expensive and time-consuming. Real estate is bought and sold in a non-auction market. It is usually highly leveraged, with owners financing most (and sometimes all) of the purchase price; some aggressive mortgage plans even offer *more* than 100 percent of equity in the form of loans. Real estate has tangible value and is owned directly by the purchaser.

The differences between these two markets make comparisons difficult. Because the varying market risks, costs, and other attributes are dissimilar, it is a mistake to apply stock market assumptions to real estate valuation.

3. *Numerous "cause-and-effect" realities affect value beyond simple supply and demand.* Everyone who has studied economics has read about the supply-and-demand cycle. This cycle operates logically and predictably in most markets. But when real supply and real demand is replaced with bubble versions of the same things (driven by greed and fear), the supply-and-demand cycle is thrown off and no longer works predictably. This aberration is always temporary, and eventually the bubble either bursts or dissipates.

In the supply-and-demand cycle, well-understood forces are at work. Increased demand forces prices upward. Development follows to meet higher demand but ultimately exceeds the level of demand; the resulting oversupply causes prices to fall or to level out. A continuous equilibrium is maintained within this "normal" supply-and-demand cycle.

Many outside factors will influence valuation of real estate. These include changes in interest rates, increased speculation, liberal and unlimited lending policies, and the *perception* among investors, homeowners, and speculators that prices are going to rise indefinitely. The resulting bubble is irrational, of course, because the belief is not supportable within the well-understood supply-and-demand cycle. The artificial demand created when speculators begin trading among themselves creates, in turn, excess supply as developers respond. As prices continue to rise, more and more new construction follows, fueled by ever-growing speculation. This form of cause and effect is self-propelling and invariably accelerates to a fever pitch until the supply of new speculators becomes exhausted.

4. *Greed and fear are the predominant emotions in all speculation.* No one will ever admit that their decision-making process is based on greed and fear. But in practice these emotions dominate bubbles. The "fever pitch" that bubbles reach right before they burst is easily seen time and again in all kinds of market bubbles. And when the prices tumble, the resulting panic is equally exaggerated.

Once you are aware that the greed-and-fear effect is always dominant in markets, you will be better able to apply logic and, in fact, exploit those emotions. This is where contrarian investing can become most profitable. For example, when real estate prices tumble following a bubble, most people become afraid to invest in real estate. However, that is precisely the time for cooler heads to prevail, when bargains can be found on the market. And when prices are rising in the most severe bubbles, there are ways to exploit that condition as well. (In Chapter 8, some additional ideas are offered for how you can exploit greed and fear to time real estate investments wisely.)

5. *Fundamental analysis works in all markets.* The study of financial strength or weakness—fundamental analysis—is a widely accepted science in the stock market. It is rarely mentioned in real estate. However, in terms of analyzing bubbles, the fundamentals are essential. The intrinsic value of property based on comparable sales, the cost of replacement (in other words,

appraisal methods), interaction between property value and market rental rates, and other real estate fundamentals help to identify the fundamental value of property. When this value is compared to current market value, a dollar amount can be placed on the bubble. It is the amount of divergence between fundamental (or, intrinsic) value and current market value.

Real estate investors are often at a loss to define how they assess real estate values. In the stock market, many fundamental tools are available. These include earnings per share, PE ratio, record of growth in revenue and earnings, and dividend yield. In real estate, the closest thing to an obvious fundamental indicator is a comparative study of cash flow, and many investors are not really certain how to quantify this. In the following sections, the various methods available for understanding valuation and identifying—for lack of a better term—the intrinsic value of real estate will help to define the extent of the bubble.

The study of valuation for nonresidential properties is key in the analysis of bubbles, because the various methods of setting value help to understand how real estate works. Even if you never invest directly in nonresidential property, it is instructive to see how various types of real property become valued at specific levels.

RETAIL PROPERTY VALUATION

Just as valuation of residential property is determined by precise market influences, retail properties also react to unique forces. However, because the characteristics of retail properties are not the same as those for residential, retail properties act differently in the market.

Location and Customer Base

Retail property value is invariably based on location and customer base, which includes potential sales volume and profit generated within one neighborhood or market. Retail valuation is broken down into four distinct segments:

1. *Trade Area.* A retail "trade area" is defined by the customer base in terms of household location in relation to the retail property. This includes economic analysis, because specific types of retail outlets appeal to specific economic groups. So trade area analysis includes a study of traffic volume (notably when studying shopping malls), compatibility between the type of retail outlet and the local demographics, and the perception among the customer base of the retail outlet image.

2. *Purchasing Power.* Retail valuation—often employed before construction of a mall or retail center—includes analysis of local population statistics, such as average income (per capita and median household income studies), size and density of population, age concentration, and other data.

3. *Market Area.* A "market area" is distinct and different from a "trade area." The trade area is defined by location of a customer base; but a market area is more involved with a study of competition and location. So valuation of retail space is determined by a study of direct competition for business within the same immediate area, of customers and how much customer base has to be shared with competing outlets, and of how demographic trends might affect retail competition in the future.

The competitive aspect of valuation can be broken down into three classifications.

   a. Generative business comes from opening retail space that will be appealing enough to draw customers directly (for example, a popular restaurant may draw customers due to image and quality, even when many competing restaurants are found in the same market area).

   b. Shared business includes the possibility of cross-selling (for example, a multiscreen cinema may draw business within a large shopping mall from people who already shop there).

c. Related business is the type that attracts business from other retail outlets (for example, an auto parts store benefits when it is located near an outlet selling classic collector cars).

4. *Economic Influence.* Not every part of town is going to react to a specific type of retail store in the same way. A store selling expensive renovation hardware would not expect to thrive in an area where most residential properties are rentals. A study of household demographics, age, and income determines the specific potential for a type of store within a neighborhood. Distance is also important in this study. People tend to shop as close as possible to where they live, so a store that is farther away from customers than a competing store will gain less market share.

Retail Bubbles

The study of retail properties can and should include an analysis of the potential for bubbles. If a particular area's population is growing rapidly, there may be a tendency to overbuild retail space. Malls are especially vulnerable to retail bubbles. In many cities, malls have been built with oversaturation of some types of stores, or have included tenants whose market simply was not strong enough to support those stores. As a consequence, such malls suffer higher than average vacancies and, ultimately, property values fall.

Factors Determining Value

In retail, property values are invariably based on analysis of profitability, cash flow, market rents, and tax incentives. So these four factors will determine value:

1. *Profitability.* Profitability in retail is not the same as that for residential. To a homeowner who buys property and later

sells it, "profit" refers to the net difference between purchase and sale prices. It is straightforward and well understood. In retail property, profitability is more complex. Retail properties (like multi-unit residential properties) are appraised based on the income a property generates. A retail mall's market value is determined by the income paid by its tenants. Chronic high vacancies translate into lower market value. So the consequence of a retail bubble is going to be depressed prices for retail space.

2. *Cash Flow.* Cash flow may be more important than profitability in determining the viability of investing in retail property. For the investor, the income from rentals has to be adequate to meet all expenses and obligations associated with the property. A shortfall (negative cash flow) can lead to disaster.

A rather flip attitude toward cash flow is seen in periods when property values are rising quickly (notably during bubble periods). The idea is that it's all right to have negative cash flow as long as property values are outpacing the dollar amount of the shortfall. This belief ignores two important types of risk. First, there is no assurance that property values will *continue* to outpace negative cash flow. Second, if the bubble does exist, the ramification is that too many retail outlets are being placed on the market, which means high vacancies in the future. The consequence there is twofold: (a) High vacancies will aggravate and increase the negative cash flow; and (b) the overbuilt conditions will cause property values to fall (a burst of the bubble) and retail investors then stand to lose everything.

3. *Value of Rental Income.* Rental income defines the market value of retail space. A "conceptual" value is not enough to establish value. Thus, an estimate that a shopping center would command market value if and when fully leased is not the bottom line. The vacancy factor is deducted and actual net rents are used to establish value under the "income approach" of appraisal. Here again, the existence of a bubble translates to higher vacancies, and thus to lower market value. In residential bubbles, real

demand dries up as more speculators place pressure to develop an oversupply of housing units. But in retail bubbles, an oversupply of retail outlets causes lower market rents and higher vacancies.

4. *Tax Incentives.* Tax incentives are more limited today than they were in the past. At one time, real estate investors could write off large losses resulting from rapid depreciation of retail property, but today, actual losses are limited. If you invest in retail property through a *passive* method (such as a limited partnership) you are not allowed to deduct losses but have to apply those losses against passive gains. The only tax incentive for real estate investors who directly participate in managing their properties (and, as a requisite, own at least 10 percent equity interest) is an allowance up to $25,000 per year in loss deductions. So tax incentives are limited for investors in any type of property, even if it is owned directly and managed personally by the investor. An exception is the full-time real estate professional, whose losses are not limited.

A longer-term tax incentive for most people is the eventual net profit from investing in real estate. Capital gains rates for properties owned more than one year are lower than federal rates charged for ordinary taxable income.

COMMERCIAL PROPERTY VALUATION

Beyond the well-known residential and retail classifications of real estate, it is also possible to invest in office and industrial property, or in lodging and tourism. Of course, there are many other real estate categories. These two areas are emphasized because they represent large segments of the overall commercial property investment in the United States. Office and industrial space, for example, accounts for 62 percent of all commercial property sales. By comparison, retail property is only 14 percent of the total.[1]

Most investors are only able to invest in big-scale properties through conduit programs like real estate partnerships or Real Estate Investment Trusts (REITs). The advantage of these products is that you can place a small amount of cash into the programs, rather than needing to obtain a large mortgage and having to make a down payment. The disadvantage is that as a passive investor, you gain no tax benefits and have no say in how properties are selected and managed.

How Bubbles Affect Office and Industrial Properties

When considering the possibilities of how real estate bubbles are likely to affect office and industrial space, you need to appreciate the overall economic risks of a specific region. For example, if a housing bubble were to burst in one city, would that also affect commercial real estate? The answer cannot be known for certain, but you can speculate as to likely outcomes.

If residential real estate values fall due to a bubble bursting, some people will lose money—possibly all of their investment capital. A catastrophic loss among speculators could have a rippling effect throughout the local economy. While greed dictates and controls bubbles as those bubbles expand, fear controls sentiment after values have fallen. So losses in the residential market could affect commercial property values as well.

There is a related economic factor to consider. As investment in residential property increases rapidly (as it does in a bubble), it is likely that office and industrial activity follows suit. When development of residential properties occurs in response to both real demand and speculative demand, it makes sense to expect greater activity in other kinds of development. So the best way to judge potential office and industrial bubble risk is by studying the markets and the volume of commercial activity by city. For example, the three largest office markets in the United States (measured by the amount of square feet of office space available) are Manhattan, Chicago, and Dallas.[2]

These three regions are among the most vulnerable in terms of residential real estate bubbles. For example, by mid-2006, the bubble in Chicago had become severe. A May 2006 article in the *Chicago Tribune* cited an alarming statistic. In the previous year, the inventory of residential property had grown from a three-year supply to a five-year supply in Chicago. The article further cautioned that the market had shifted from a hot price market:

> What has changed in terms of verifiable statistics is that the inventory of homes on the market has surged, even for traditional spring selling season. Faced with so much competition, many sellers are being counseled to settle in for a longer wait, and think hard about their asking price.[3]

If Chicago's residential market began a downward trend in real estate that culminated in a multiyear supply of housing by 2006—which the numbers appear to support—then office and industrial trends are likely to follow. Because Chicago was the country's second-largest office space market in recent years, the ramifications of an overall decline in residential values may easily spill over into the commercial side as well.

Similar concerns would apply to any market with large investment in office space. Manhattan is especially vulnerable. In New York City and surrounding communities, residential property values have risen faster than most areas, and the city is vulnerable to a bursting bubble. A residential change would be likely to also affect office values, even in so large and diverse a market.

Office space is not the only vulnerable market; industrial space is equally likely to suffer from a residential price decliner. For example, Chicago has been by far the largest market for industrial properties, with over one billion square feet of industrial space, more than twice as much industrial property as any other city in the United States.

Factors Determining Value

For office and industrial properties, an analysis of the attributes defining value is helpful in determining the likelihood of vulnerability to a residential bubble. The primary factors include:

1. *Class of Building.* The most attractive investment properties are Class A, which include the most modern and updated properties. An area with large percentages of Class B or C properties is likely to be more vulnerable than one with a greater portion of Class A buildings.

2. *Location and Size.* Location and size define value, not only for office and industrial space but for all classifications of property. However, important distinctions in commercial property include comparisons between overall space and rentable space, which may be important in older buildings, where the non-rentable portion may be greater than average.

3. *Amenities.* Amenities of a building include space on each floor or design of space on a single level. Design elements may vary in importance depending on the type of tenant.

4. *Obsolescence.* Obsolescence also determines value of commercial properties. In older buildings, columns impede views and use of floor space, and internal systems are likely to be inefficient in comparison with better-designed, more thoroughly insulated, and more modern properties.

How Bubbles Affect Lodging and Tourism Properties

Another important subclassification of commercial property is that of lodging and tourism. As with other commercial projects, most investors are likely to be involved with these types of properties through pooled investments, such as REITs or partnerships.

Lodging and tourism are especially sensitive to seasonal changes and to economic impact. With this in mind, it is also apparent that any fallout from residential bubbles will probably have an *immediate* effect on lodging and tourism. The negative real estate news in a particular area is going to affect many types of property. And when you consider the attributes of valuation in this type of real estate, it becomes apparent that lodging and tourism properties are probably more vulnerable than most.

In studying potential bubble fallout for the lodging and tourism industry, you need to remember that this is a segment that is exceptionally sensitive to economic changes. So whenever consumer sentiment responds to negative news (interest rate hikes, higher unemployment, etc.), the lodging industry is affected directly. If a particularly severe bubble is about to burst and make big news, consumers will become apprehensive about housing and, by association, everything else. Fear is contagious. So if property values fall in your area, you are going to be less likely to take an expensive vacation.

This is an extrapolation and an oversimplification, of course. But the element of uncertainty is very real. The lodging industry is not as much a creature of supply and demand as it is of "supply and desire." The simple desire to take vacations and to travel (both for personal reasons and for business) is well understood. One segment of the lodging business also involves business travel and conventions. However, when businesses are concerned about their bottom lines, they are less likely to spend money to send employees to seminars and conventions or even to sponsor their own annual sales meetings at the same expense levels as in "better times."

Factors Determining Value

In summary, the lodging industry responds to many conditions, both real and perceived, beyond the demand for facilities. Key factors that affect value for lodging properties include:

1. *Location.* Within the lodging industry, subgroups include physical and market location. Physical locations are broadly di-

vided into three groups: downtown, convention, and travel (airport and roadside). Markets include business, vacation/leisure, and corporate (these are the major groups, but many subgroups also exist).

2. *Season.* Most segments of the lodging industry (and the entire tourism segment) are clearly seasonal. Even the rather large convention subgroup tends to be most active in spring and fall, for example. The transportation industry (airlines, rail, and car rentals) has its peak seasons, and the lodging industry seasonal variation mirrors the cyclical trends in transportation at large.

3. *Amenities.* Every market within this segment can be specifically defined by the theme presented to guests. For example, the Las Vegas market used to feature just gaming, but today is additionally characterized by sports amenities and, in many hotels, by family-oriented themes. Markets in Orlando, Florida, have to include family-oriented amenities because of the high volume of theme park travelers. And the New York professional market has to ensure ready availability for meeting space, fine dining, and (in the larger hotels catering to business travelers) features like expanded business centers.

4. *Competitive Forces.* In the lodging and tourism industry, competition is not limited to similar properties. It also has to take into account the fact that customers have choices in destination and in how and where they spend their money. A basic assumption in the residential property market is that everyone who is looking for property needs to buy. But in lodging and tourism, people have many choices besides staying in one of several hotels in a downtown area. They may choose to go elsewhere. Even defining a "market area" within the lodging industry is elusive because the customer base is a moving target. In the convention segment, it is not reasonable to assume that convention business will come to one of three possible convention hotels in one city; based on price and convenience, convention business may go to an entirely different city.

5. *Specific Demand Variables.* The level of demand in most types of real estate is fairly easy to distinguish. Even when a bubble dominates the market, the existing real demand is defined by levels of recent sales. So if 400 homes sell per month, the "real demand" in the local market is 4,800 units per year. If there are 24,000 properties available today, that is a five-year supply.

In lodging and tourism, demand is more elusive than in residential markets. Some market analysts have erred in estimating likely demand for a proposed new hotel complex by assuming that 100 percent of future real demand will be absorbed by the project, and ignoring the reality that the project will receive only a share of the overall market—and that share cannot be known with any certainty.

Lodging demand is invariably defined by the type of guest involved. This definition includes the purpose of a trip (business, convention, vacation, sports, or one-night stay during road travel); time of the typical stay (highway properties normally have a guest stay for only one night, while convention attendees stay for the specific number of nights required for attendance); and subtle amenity-based determinations (a guest might choose one property over another because it offers a free breakfast, a location with easy access to the freeway, free transportation to the airport, or a 24-hour café on the premises).

A detailed study of a property's direct competition is exceptionally complex in comparison to other classifications of real estate because of the many variables (price, season, amenities, guest attributes, transportation available, nearby restaurants, entertainment, and attractions).

Impact of Regional Bubbles

The potential for valuation of lodging and tourism properties to be affected by changes in residential bubbles is uncertain. Without any doubt, these properties are highly sensitive to any economic changes, because those changes affect travel volume itself. When people are fearful about the economy in general, they tend to travel less. If a particular region experiences an end to the rise in housing prices—and the bubble bursts—it will have an immediate impact, even though that impact itself cannot be specifically defined. So, for example, if Florida real estate goes into a virtual standstill, will that affect tourism in southern Florida? Or, more likely, will it cause residents living and working in southern Florida to travel less to other regions?

These concerns would certainly be on the minds of a corporation investing in lodging and tourism properties, or of investors placing capital into REITs and other pooled real estate investments. However, the actual impact of a regional bubble's bursting is highly uncertain, even when the impact would be immediate and very real on some segment of the lodging and tourism market.

VALUATION OF RAW LAND

A final classification of real estate worth studying is raw land. In fact, land speculation itself has had a long history in the United States, and so have land swindles. The classic example of inexperienced investors buying Florida swamp land is so well known that it has taken on the proportion of an urban legend. However, land swindles of all kinds have occurred and continue to occur. But even diligent research into land values cannot ensure wise selection for speculators. Many variables go into identification of sound investment.

Three Kinds of Raw Land

Raw land can be generally classified into three groups.

1. *Building Lots for Which Essential Services Are Nearby or Even Immediate.* Thus, water, sewer, and electrical

hook-ups exist across the street and will require connections only. Cities and towns usually charge a permit fee for hooking up to these services and that is part of the cost of constructing homes on lots. So typically, these lots are in close proximity to existing improved lots, and their price reflects the existence of those utilities. For obvious reasons, the lot with services readily available will reflect full market value for raw land.

2. *Building Lots That Do Not Offer Essential Services in the Immediate Vicinity.* Electrical, water, and sewer hook-ups might be close by, and some buyers may consider this to be an easy problem to overcome. However, when the typical building lot in town is $115,000 and a lot just out of town is only $10,000, don't jump at the opportunity. It is virtually certain that the difference reflects the cost that will be involved in running utilities from their current location to the lot.

3. *Building Lots That Are Truly Raw.* There are no water or sewer hook-ups nearby. Construction will require drilling a well or joining a local water association, and installing a septic system. If the area is primarily rural, electrical service is probably available, but is likely to be far more expensive than services in town.

Buying Raw Land

Anyone trying to place value on raw land should be aware of these inhibiting factors, all of which will be reflected in current market value. Not only initial cost but the cost of on-going utilities (as well as quality and promptness of service) should be factored into the buying decision.

The ideal time to invest in raw land is when development is on the way but is not yet just around the corner. Identify the path of development; then locate land that is for sale and that is most likely to increase in value when development does occur.

The challenge is to make this identification before everyone else realizes it as well—and that is where the risk element enters the picture. First, you might be wrong about the path of progress; it may change course and move away from that raw land you bought. Second, you have no control over the timing of development. Even with announced plans for expanding residential areas and city boundaries, the decision by one large employer to close a plant can bring plans to a grinding halt, and progress may stop indefinitely.

Raw Land Bubbles

Bubbles can and do occur in raw land. Bubbles come into existence with raw land on the basis of rumors. For example, you may hear a rumor that the Disney Corporation is going to build a new theme park outside of Fairport, South Dakota (about 50 miles northeast of Rapid City and in the middle of nowhere). Although this makes no sense, it is possible that some people, upon hearing the rumor, will impulsively begin buying up cheap land in the area, in the belief that they will make a fortune. A "land grab" can take on panic proportions for many reasons, including rumors of a new gold strike, plans to develop new recreational outlets (theme parks, casinos, etc.), or even ideas like construction of large subdivisions.

If enough people believe these rumors and begin buying up raw land, the greed factor may attract more and more people, and the interest itself may drive up land values. This raw land bubble can even continue for many months, but if the rumors turn out to be untrue or premature, many people can lose money.

The rumors don't have to be untrue, either; even actual plans may be delayed indefinitely, causing land values to tumble. For example, in the nineteenth century, a huge land bubble occurred in Chicago when plans were announced to build a new canal. The idea made absolute sense because the canal would connect Chicago to the East Coast by water. Had that occurred in the original time frame, Chicago land values would have remained high. Instead, plans were deferred an entire decade, so that the fast run-up in land values turned into a fiasco. Values fell once the canal plans were put off, and many people lost their fortunes due to premature land speculation. Ultimately, the canal was built, and it led to Chicago's rapid growth. The city became (and remained) the major economic center of the Midwest. But for the land speculators, the fast run-up in values had been followed quickly by a complete collapse.

Raw land speculation is by no means an easy way to make money in real estate. The risks are far greater than the simple risk of being swindled into buying useless swamp land. Even actual planned events can be changed due to outside causes (such as the case of Chicago when the planned canal was delayed due to economic conditions). But unfortunately, the solution is not to find a qualified expert to advise you. In fact, no land speculation or investment can be assured to be successful by hiring someone to advise you. It may work in the stock market, although the history of investment advice is dismal even there. But certainly, real estate investors invariably end up performing their own market research and finding their own bargains.

Chapter 7 provides guidelines for finding well-priced real estate and avoiding the mistake of buying at the top of the bubble.

NOTES

1. CoStar Market Report as of first quarter of 2002.
2. New York (Manhattan) reported over 300 million square feet of office space, Chicago nearly 250 million square feet, and Dallas over 200 million square feet. Source: Society of Industrial and Office Realtors, 2004.
3. Mary Umberger, "It's a Buyer's Market," *Chicago Tribune*, May 7, 2006.

C H A P T E R 7

Be Your Own Market Analyst

The real estate market is huge, with millions of investors, homeowners, and speculators involved. Millions more specialists—real estate brokers and salespeople, appraisers, assessors, escrow agents, title companies, inspectors, publishers, online experts, investment companies, and lenders—are further involved in offering services for a fee.

Even though the real estate industry is so huge, there are few real estate market analysts available to advise you as an investor. Although some people may position themselves as experts, they are invariably in the business for a profit and cannot possibly offer you *objective* advice. Financial planners are oriented toward mutual funds in most instances. And real estate agents focus on closing sales and are not usually qualified to offer expert advice.

This means you are on your own: You will have to be your own market analyst.

THE THREE KINDS OF REAL ESTATE OWNERS

In entering real estate in any of three general categories, your purchases will be the largest you will ever make, but objective advice does not really exist. This is true in each classification of investment:

1. *Homeowners.* The historical trend in home ownership has been strong and growing for many decades. By the end of 2005, approximately 60 percent of all families owned their own home. For the decade ending in 2005, the number of housing units grew steadily, as shown in Figure 7-1.[1]

Homeowners view property ownership far differently from investors or speculators. Thus it is a mistake to assume that by virtue of owning a home, you already understand the risk aspects

Figure 7-1. Number of housing units in the United States: 1996 to 2005.

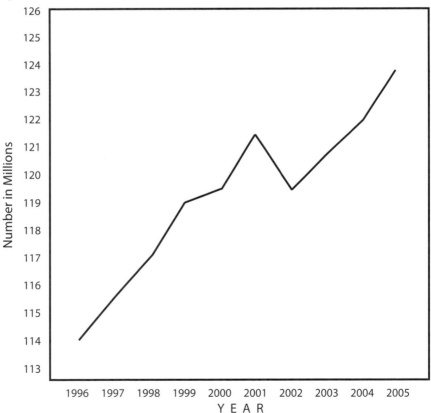

Source: U.S. Census Bureau.

to the real estate market. Home ownership is a relatively safe investment, because the family lives on the property: It is monitored daily, it is insured, and the interest and property tax expenses are tax deductible, so that the gross cost of a mortgage is subsidized through tax benefits.

Homeowners may experience bubbles like all real estate owners. However, if the purpose of living in a particular house is long term, you may not be immediately concerned or aware of gyrations in market value. More important are the questions every homeowner faces: affordability of the mortgage, proximity to schools and jobs, quality of local education, safety, and quality of life.

2. *Investors.* The investor's point of view toward real estate is vastly different from that of the homeowner. While investors may also be homeowners, it would be a mistake for a first-time landlord-to-be to assume that buying investment property is the same as buying a family home. As an investor, you need to be far more concerned with the details of financing, tenant review, cash flow, and taxes.

Risks for owner-occupied housing are far less than for investment property, so lenders apply more stringent requirements to investors. For example, most lenders demand higher down payments from investors than from homeowners, and the interest rate is often higher as well.

Tenant review ultimately determines whether your experience as an investor is going to be positive or negative. Finding a responsible tenant is crucial for ensuring that rent will be paid on time and that the property will be cared for properly. This includes a rental application and review of credit, employment, and references; a very specific rental contract; and a carefully documented summary of everything in the house, its condition, and any flaws at the time the tenant moves in.

As an investor, cash flow is more important to you than eventual profitability. If cash flow is negative or minimal, it does not take much to make an investment unprofitable. Cash flow should include not only deductible expenses but also consideration for nondeductible payments (capital expenditures and payment of the principal portion of the mortgage) as well as noncash expenses (for depreciation). Net cash flow should also take into account the tax benefits in investing in real estate.

Taxes often make the difference between negative cash flow and after-tax positive cash flow. The feasibility of buying and owning investment real estate is completely different from owning your own home. For homeowners, the big question is whether the mortgage payment is affordable; the potential profit in home ownership is relatively unimportant. For investors, the emphasis is different because, ideally, payments should be covered from rental income.

3. *Speculators.* Unlike homeowners and investors, speculators are short-term real estate players. They are often one of the three driving forces behind bubbles (the others being developers and lenders). Developers gladly respond to speculative demand (even when real demand has been exceeded), especially if payment is readily offered. Lenders gladly finance the interaction between developers and speculators, because the secondary market provides a virtual unlimited funding source. (You will recall that the secondary market agencies report stockholders' equity averages under 2 percent of their loan guarantees. If this ratio were applied to other corporations, it would be alarming that such a low degree of overall capitalization was represented by equity, and that such a large portion was on the books in the form of debt.)[2]

Speculators participate in bubbles in several ways. The property flip involves buying and selling property in a very short term, often accomplished without ever actually acquiring title. For example, a speculator enters a contract to purchase a property that has not yet been started, arranges financing, and then finds a buyer at a higher price. The actual close on the property may take place during construction, with the speculator netting a good profit in the property flip. Some speculators are confident about the lifespan of a bubble and actually take possession, waiting out double-digit growth rates and then finding a buyer after two to three months have passed.

The property flip is very popular in the preconstruction market in condos, especially in Miami-Dade. It has been a practice in the recent past for many speculators, developers, and lenders to drive the market values up ever higher. This trend continues in the bubble phenomenon until the supply of new speculators becomes exhausted.

REACTING TO BUBBLE CHALLENGES

In looking for and identifying bubbles, you face a number of challenges. All of these challenges are based on the natural tendency to react to markets with the two dominant emotions of fear and greed. These apply in virtually every possible situation, including the following:

1. *You currently own your home.* As a homeowner, you serve your own interests well by keeping a clear distinction between personal assets and investments. Your home is your family's cornerstone, probably your largest asset, and the basis for security and stability. Most families become rooted in their communities in ways that exceed the size of their lot and the square footage of their homes. Children bond with friends and socialize within their schools. Parents find jobs and activities, make friends, and use their home as the base for every aspect of their lives. When a homeowner begins to react to market forces, often out of fear, all of this is at jeopardy.

If your intention is to remain in your home for the indefinite future, it is a mistake to begin thinking like a speculator. As bad as greed is as an emotion, fear is worse. With greed, a homeowner might be tempted to take profits today, before the bubble bursts. With fear, a homeowner may panic and sell, thinking values are going to fall. But these are speculator emotions, and homeowners may damage themselves and their families by responding to them.

Moving purely for financial reasons and in response to either greed or fear is a bad idea. As long as you can afford your mortgage, enjoy living in your home, and don't want to move, it makes sense for you to ignore the housing market—even if the current value appears to be the result of a bubble.

2. *You are holding rental properties.* Investors face a different problem from homeowners. Most residential property investors enter into ownership with two initial assumptions: first, cash flow will be adequate to cover expenses and payments, and second, property values will rise over time and create profits.

If either of these assumptions proves untrue, then the venture can turn into a costly financial mistake. So from the investor's point of view, focus must be on feasibility of immediate cash flow and intermediate or long-term profits. If either of these requirements is not being met, it could make sense to sell property and cut losses rather than allowing the situation to continue indefinitely. Just as a stock investor is smart to take a short-term loss to avoid a larger loss down the road, real estate investors need to accept reality, and reduce losses whenever possible.

If, as a real estate investor, you find yourself in a bubble—especially if the evidence is convincing—you should consider selling property as quickly as possible. The alternative of reverting to speculator status, hoping to ride out the bubble as far as possible, is both dangerous and reckless. An investor cannot afford to put equity at risk by getting greedy. It is wiser to sell as soon as the bubble becomes apparent to avoid disastrous losses in the near future.

If you find yourself fully invested in property whose value has fallen suddenly, it will be tempting to sell right away out of fear, hoping to avoid further losses. But as long as cash flow continues to cover all of the on-going expenses and payment obligations, don't be in a rush to dump the property. If you are a long-term investor, the bursting of a bubble is a problem, but a well-selected property will eventually recover and regain its lost market value.

3. *There is some question as to whether the bubble is real.* There may be uncertainty as to the existence of a bubble in your area. Some of the arguments are primarily academic, challenging the very idea that bubbles exist at all. For example, under the efficient market hypothesis (which holds that all prices are fair because "the market" has all the information it needs to establish value), the concept of bubble valuation is deemed impossible.

The problem with the efficient market hypothesis is that it is not always applicable. When an area has a current inventory of houses greater than two years, it is clear that too many properties are for sale. When that supply reaches five years or more and prices are continuing to rise, it is evident that those prices are *not* being driven by real demand. Clearly, anyone who is invested in properties should track the inventory and, as it inches up, would be well advised to sell long before it reaches a five-year level. On the other side of this equation, recognizing an excessive demand is one way to avoid investing in the first place and overpaying for inflated properties.

It is indisputable that bubbles do exist; you must determine for yourself whether your area is in the midst of one. When you hear any extreme argument (either that you should sell your house immediately or that there is no bubble) you need to consider the source. Invariably, the source or person making the argument has some underlying reason for doing so. For example, it may be a website promoting exchange among speculators, advising you that there is no bubble. The person running that website is making a living from the commissions and fees involved in high-volume exchanges of property, and so would naturally argue that there is nothing to worry about.

Bubbles are real, but they are not universal. And when they burst in one area or for one type of property, it will not affect all types of real estate in all regions. There is no substitute for analyzing the key factors for your area to arrive at your own conclusions. Remember too that just because markets are efficient does not mean they are perfect.

4. *Speculative opportunities are tempting because property values are growing in double digits in your city.* When you witness ever-higher real estate prices, it is difficult to resist the temptation to jump onto the trend. Because other people are speculating and making easy money, by staying out of the real estate market you are losing the opportunity. It appears that prices are going to rise forever.

Every speculator who goes into the market begins with this rationale. Greed is a strong influence on people and their thought processes. But as attractive as opportunities seem to be, you cannot ignore the risk factor. Because you have no idea when the bubble will burst, any money you put into a bubble economy is at great risk. The only thing that is certain is that the bubble will burst suddenly and unexpectedly, and that someone—the person who owns property at that moment—is going to lose everything. You don't want that someone to be you.

5. *You have been offered a "sure thing."* Although everyone knows—logically—that there are no sure things, it is easy to respond to such offers emotionally. People are easily swayed by the promise of easy and fast wealth. The temptation should always be avoided, however, in recognition of some basic truths: Money is never earned without work, a sure thing may be quite expensive, and if there were any sure things no one would be spreading the word about them.

MANAGING GREED AND FEAR

Any logical analysis of market behavior cannot possibly capture the actual *mood* that dominates investment decisions. Greed and fear are extremely strong emotions and, when in their grip, people do not make wise choices. They tend to react without rationale or analysis.

Exceptional changes in markets are characterized with words like "panic" and "mania" for good reason. They are extreme in the sense that people act in extreme ways, often contrary to their best interests. Any attempt to understand real estate bubbles logically is going to be limited for this reason. One academic study observed that a purely mathematical attempt to explain bubbles is flawed, because "in many cases the correspondence between the mathematical entities and the phenomenon they are supposed to model is likely to be tenuous."[3]

Any analysis of greed and fear is best done by observing specific behavior within times of bubbles and crashes, and not with the application of mathematical modeling. Even if you find comfort in the efficient market hypothesis, it remains true that at times when greed and fear dominate, the hypothesis does not rule behavior. For those with a purely academic approach to real estate, this reality is not comforting. In fact, it is quite disturbing. Anyone who relies on rational thought processes is going to be at a loss to explain how greed and fear can completely overtake not only the market itself, but the people exchanging money within the market.

The Power of Greed

Greed overtakes and destroys logic. It creates the illusion within a person's brain that an opportunity is present, but it ignores the corresponding risk. In the early 1980s, when the price of gold ran up to over $800 per ounce, many people were investing money in gold coins in the belief that the price was going to continue rising indefinitely. Greed had taken over. A logical examination of gold prices would have led an analytical person to conclude that a quick price run-up is never sustained but tends to correct after a period of time. This gold bubble was short-lived and many people (some of whom even borrowed money to invest in gold bullion, coins, or stock) lost quite a bit of money.

The outcome of acting on greed is often loss, and for good reason. When investment decisions are made based on greed, it actually becomes difficult to sell and take profits at some point; greed tends to become stronger as prices continue rising. At the point that prices do turn and fall—which usually happens quite suddenly and always unexpectedly—those investors who acted based on greed lose their paper profits, and more.

The efficient market hypothesis sounds logical in the abstract, but it is based on two important underlying assumptions—that all investors act in a rational manner *and* that they consider all available information when making decisions. "Available" information for a bubble includes oversupply of housing in multiple-year increments, the rate of increases in prices, and ominous danger signs such as increasing foreclosure and default rates. In the height of a bubble, these signals are not only easily overlooked—they are ignored intentionally because greed dominates the decision-making process.

Bubble Behavior Is Not Rational

An observation of market behavior also reveals that investors tend to put great emphasis on recent events, and much less emphasis on past events. In a bubble, *recent* events include rapidly increasing market value, so a tendency is to believe that this trend is on-going without end. At the same time, investors may overlook and even forget more remote experiences in the market, including actual loss due to poor timing or reacting to greed. As a general observation, a truth concerning greed can be stated as:

> Humans tend to place the greatest weight on recent events. When markets perform well, they expect the trend to continue.

Even the most conservative investors abandon rational concerns over risk when it appears that easy profits can be earned. Self-programming in this environment works against profit-taking, because greed tells people to constantly wait for *more* profits. Consequently, investing in a bubble often leads people to place more capital at risk, placing greater amounts of money into the market, and even borrowing money to increase future profits. Of course, when bubbles crash, this means not only that paper profits disappear, but that speculators end up in debt.

The oddity of how people behave when greed dominates the thought process is based on broad generalizations in thought. Ideas like "This is a sure thing" or "I have to get my share of the profits" or "Real estate will remain hot forever" are not only false, they are irrational. So when it appears that easy profits are available, rational thought is sacrificed.

There are three themes that dominate "behavioral finance" and explain the poor judgment shown during bubbles. First is "heuristics," the idea that people tend to make decisions based on rule-of-thumb rather than detailed analysis. Second is "framing," which describes the way that people actually make decisions (often based on how questions are posed rather than on an analysis of actual risks). Third is "inefficiency," which explains how irrational expectations affect decisions.[4]

These three themes help to explain behavior within bubbles, underscoring the idea that people are acting on greed rather than on logic. For example, an investor may buy into the idea that "Everyone knows housing prices always go up" (*heuristics*). A speculator may attract new speculators by asking, "Don't you want to make money in real estate?" (*framing*). And in observing recent price trends, an investor might conclude that in spite of fundamental signs of a weakening market, "I will certainly be able to time my decisions to leave the market *right before* the bubble bursts," when in fact no one has ever been able to perfectly time an exit, because it is not observable until it is too late (*inefficiency*).

Fear Is the Flip Side of Greed

Fear is just as strong as greed, but it enters the picture after a bubble has burst. As prices fall, fear sets in and those speculators with the most at risk—those who have been the most greedy—tend to experience the greatest fear, at times for good reason. If a speculator has turned profits over into larger positions, mortgaged their homes to invest even more money, and sold other assets to put as much as possible into real estate, a drastic fall in prices is, indeed, disastrous.

Even if investors have only modest holdings, fear is going to be irrational. So a homeowner, fearing the consequences of a bubble bursting, might sell her home when the market is perfectly balanced and no actual bubble exists. After a bubble does burst in a different region or with another type of property, it is equally possible that an individual will make rash decisions out of fear rather than as the result of logic.

Many attributes of fear are similar to those of greed. In fact, looking at investor behavior, it is easy to conclude that greed and fear affect people in a similar manner, the primary distinction being the mental state. During periods when people are acting out of greed, their irrational optimism clouds judgment. During periods characterized by fear, the dread of loss is equally compromising. But the outcome is similar in the fact that during both extremes, people act illogically.

This is the universal fact about fear:

> When market values fall, people panic and become convinced that the trend will continue forever. They move quickly to cut losses, even when they don't need to.

The efficient market hypothesis can be useful in the analysis of investment behavior, but it should be used only as a starting point. The reality about bubbles is that, as a basic characteristic, logic is thrown aside and replaced by greed and fear. A reasonable person who has speculated in real estate might be able to extricate capital from a real estate investment, take profits, and avoid trouble; but when markets are falling, it is less likely that a speculator will keep a cool head and adopt a contrarian point of view. Fear leads to extreme fear, or panic, and it is less likely at such times that people with capital at risk will act in a rational way. The efficient market hypothesis is flawed in this respect, because it assumes that everyone acts rationally, in *all* markets and at *all* times.

TEN STRATEGIES FOR TAKING AN OBJECTIVE APPROACH

Whether your local real estate market is in a bubble or not, you can avoid costly mistakes by maintaining your objectivity, looking for the right kinds of information, and making *informed* decisions rather than emotional ones. Follow these recommendations:

1. *Recognize the signs of greed and fear.* Emotional reactions to markets are easy to recognize, if only because they are irrational. Greed and fear are both blind emotions in the sense that when in their grip, people do not think straight. In times of greed, people ignore risk and want to put *more* money into a venture, even when warning signs are evident. In times of fear, people just want to get out, even if that isn't necessary.

2. *Resist the natural tendency to react hastily.* To avoid the common problems that come from making decisions in response to greed and fear, never act rashly. Gather facts and think first, and be aware that most people overreact and make decisions impulsively. The old stock market advice to "buy low and sell high" clearly makes sense; the actual tendency is for people to do the exact opposite. Greed causes people to buy high, and fear causes them to sell low.

3. *Look at the big picture and ignore events in the moment.* Whenever markets are uncertain—and especially due to

valuation bubbles—it makes sense to resist acting or reacting in the moment. Take a step back, look at the market in historical perspective, and never make decisions quickly. Most mistakes in markets (real estate and others) are made because people have used the wrong justifications to act. For example, if you hear that the market for condos has taken a big hit in a region 1,000 miles from where you live, that will not affect the market value of your single-family home. In fact, a condo bubble right in your town is unlikely to have any long-lasting effects on the rest of the market.

Just as different types of real estate react to completely different supply and demand forces, the same holds true within each type of real estate. In residential property groups, single-family owner-occupied housing is entirely separate from single-family rentals, duplexes, condos, and apartment buildings. Sudden changes in markets are likely to affect all types of real estate short term, but over time the separation of supply and demand forces within markets insulate each type of property from other types.

4. *Use real estate fundamentals to judge markets.* It is all too easy to look only at market price and to ignore other factors. But when you compare current value to real demand, you get insights about the degree of artificial demand within your local market. Studying the key fundamentals—inventory of properties for sale, time on the market, and spread between asked and sold prices—reveals what is really going on today. Price and recent historical price trends can be misleading.

5. *Consider the sources of information.* Any time you receive information about real estate, consider where that information comes from. Is an organization in the business of serving speculators, investors, and other property owners? What sources of income may affect the person's or organization's reasons for giving you advice? Once you understand why someone believes something about real estate values, you are in a better position to evaluate the quality of his suggestions.

6. *Set goals and take profits based on a plan.* All investment programs work best when part of a comprehensive plan. How much of your capital should be invested in real estate? How does your family's house fit into the plan? What are your goals for paying off mortgages? Do you want to be a landlord? All of these questions form the basis for your personal financial plan.

Too many people proceed with investments without first formulating specific investing goals. Real estate, which is illiquid compared to the stock market, should represent only a portion of your total investment assets. What is the appropriate portion for you depends on how much risk you can afford to take, your income and other assets, and your knowledge of the real estate market.

7. *Seek objective advice, and be aware that financial planning should be your job and not that of someone you pay.* An entire industry of "financial planners" provides services in return for commissions, professional fees, or both. These services are promoted to help you to invest your money to plan for your future. Too many people rely on a financial planner's advice without looking into alternatives themselves. This leads to an inclination to make poor decisions. Many financial planners simply refer their clients to mutual funds that include a sales commission fee, without any guarantees that the funds will perform well.

If you check with a financial planner concerning possible real estate investments, you will discover that many planners will *not* recommend you invest in this market. First of all, it ties up a lot of capital, meaning less money is available for investments that provide the planner with a commission. Second, most financial planners do not understand the real estate market well enough to give you practical advice.

8. *Never put all of your investment capital into a single market.* The concept of diversification is well understood in the stock market. However, in discussions of real estate management, the question rarely comes up in the sense of *product* diver-

sification (real estate versus stocks, bonds, mutual funds, and savings). Diversification may be studied in terms of liquidity, with highly liquid savings accounts compared with stocks or mutual funds and real estate as different markets. But little if anything is usually brought up about whether a specific portion of investment capital should be invested in real estate in order to diversify risks.

A related concept—*asset allocation*—does compare dissimilar markets. Many formulas have been devised to recommend to investors that a certain percentage of capital should be placed in the stock market, real estate, or the money market. These discussions are rarely based on a logical comparison of risks; condition of the real estate market; the suggested method for placing money into the market; or an analysis of how a personal home should be included in the equation. In other words, asset allocation models may be affected by real or perceived real estate bubbles, but the recommendations put forth by brokerage firms or financial planners are often general in nature and not geared toward any one individual. And the reasoning for how money should be invested is not usually explained in terms of risk and profit potential.

9. *Keep personal and investment assets separate.* There is little justification for using your personal home to try and make a profit in the market, especially if you want to speculate. The suggestion that you keep personal and investment assets separate is based on the requirements that lead most people to own their own home. Profit potential is usually secondary to the more important roots in the community (schools, friends, location) and affordability of a mortgage—in other words, the very attributes that define personal security. In comparison, investment assets are intentionally put at risk, in the full knowledge that greater profit potential is always accompanied by greater risks.

10. *Learn from your mistakes. Better yet, learn from mistakes made by other people.* Smart investors learn from the

expensive mistakes they make along the way. Wise investors are able to avoid making expensive mistakes by learning from the mistakes made by others. To succeed in real estate, observe how people act within the market. Make a clear distinction between home ownership, equity investing, and speculation. These three are not the same, and money should not be placed at risk in the same way for any of the three methods of entering the market.

It's worth remembering that homeowners, investors, and speculators—as the three primary equity owners of real estate—face their own unique risks and profit opportunities, and these are not the same for all. Even beyond these methods for owning real estate, there exists a range of many more ways to invest in real estate in the forms of either equity or debt. (Chapter 8 looks at these methods and explores the possibility of using alternative investment methods to profit even when real estate prices are falling.)

Additionally, in becoming a wise investor and observing the mistakes made by others, learn to read the market. Be aware that real estate consists of three distinct submarkets, and that tracking these can help you to spot bubbles and emerging trends.

MANAGING THE THREE SUBMARKETS

The real estate market often is perceived as an easily understood, rather simple market with clear supply-and-demand elements, manageable risks, and predictable profits. Especially in comparison to the more glamorous, high-risk aspects of the stock market, real estate looks like a "sure thing." But it is far from certain that everyone buying real estate can make quick profits in double digits and avoid the risks of sudden and significant price declines.

When real estate bubbles burst, people are going to lose money, and these losses will be sudden and in many cases, large. Once speculators find out that the bubble has ended, it will be too late. In spite of commonly held beliefs to the contrary, speculators do not see the pending price changes; it becomes evident only after the changes have occurred.

There are many ways to analyze local markets to determine if a bubble exists; if so, which types of property are affected; the degree of the bubble when mixed in with real demand; and the likelihood that the bubble will burst soon. You can augment your analysis of the local real estate market by further understanding the three submarkets of real estate and by breaking down your analysis into these three components. They are the supply-and-demand market, the financing market, and the rental market (described in detail in Chapter 1). Following is a discussion about how the attributes in each of these markets may be used to spot bubbles and to anticipate the bursting of those bubbles.

The Supply-and-Demand Market

The *supply-and-demand market* is the most obvious submarket. Isolating this from other submarkets makes sense, even though most people do not attempt to break out these different markets or to study them specifically. The essential point in defining and studying bubbles with supply and demand in mind is to distinguish between real demand and artificial demand. You can use real estate fundamentals to accomplish this.

For example, if you assume that a "reasonable" supply of housing stock currently for sale is a six-month supply (based on the most recent home sales per month), then you have a benchmark for understanding the health of the market today. The six-month supply is not a hard-and-fast number because it should depend on historical sales activity. So if the market has been robust, you might want to stretch the supply number higher.

Once you have decided on the inventory benchmark, the next step is to study the current inventory of the same property type. This is an important distinction. If a bubble has been building in the condo market but not in single-family housing, it is not accurate to lump all residential property into the same group; averaging would only distort your analysis. So assuming you are studying single-family housing to decide whether or not there is a bubble and, if so, how severe it is, compare the benchmark inventory to actual inventory. If your benchmark is six months and you discover that there is a current inventory of twenty-four months, it means you can define the bubble. Of the entire current inventory, 25 percent (six months) is accounted for by real demand; the remaining 75 percent is a response to artificial demand and is the bubble inventory.

Is that a severe overage? Here again, the subjective conclusion you reach about the severity of the bubble has two components. First is the months of excess inventory; second is the trend in actual completed sales. If prices are rising and the larger trend has been toward population increases, the bubble may actually anticipate growing demand. This is not as negative a bubble as one that continues without any reason, when the real demand market has been left far behind. So you can conclude from such a study that bubbles come in many shapes and sizes, and some are actually likely to be part of the market's "demand anticipation." This is not unhealthy because in such instances, excess inventory may actually hold prices down or minimize price growth, acting as a form of local inflation check. So ironically, excess inventory within reason could prevent a bubble from going out of control.

The Financing Market

The *financing market* has caused many bubbles since the early 1970s, when the secondary market was formed. Before that, commercial lenders were restricted in the dollar value of their loan portfolios based on their actual reserves—a "sensible" system because monetary policy was tied to the gold standard in a very real sense. When the United States went off the gold standard, the entire concept of monetary policy changed. As discussed earlier, since the early 1970s the Federal Reserve can print up as much money as it wants. It is no coincidence that at the same time the United States went off the gold standard, the secondary market in real estate was formed.

In 1975, the total dollar value of U.S. home mortgages was $38.8 billion; by the end of 2005, outstanding mortgages were nearly 30 times higher, at over $1.1 trillion.[5] The trend for the decade from 1995 to 2005 showed unrelenting growth, from $168 billion at the beginning of the period, as summarized in Figure 7-2.

Does this translate to a financing bubble? It does, but the expansion of credit by itself does not imply that there is going to be a massive burst. In this respect, credit expansion is not the same kind of bubble as the pricing bubble of real estate. There is no doubt that liberal availability of money has enabled the price bubble to grow, in some areas without limit. But a bubble burst

Figure 7-2. Dollar volume of U.S. home mortgages outstanding: 1995 to 2005.

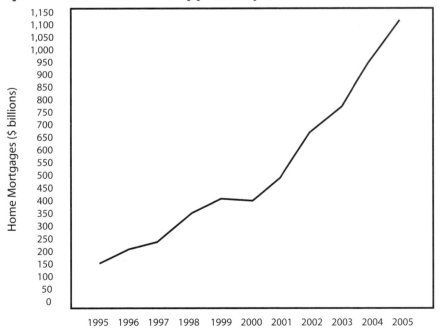

Source: Federal Reserve Board, *Flow of Funds Reports*.

is going to be experienced in price and not in some reversal of lending policy.

The early warning signs that the pricing bubble is exhausting itself can be seen within the financing market. The signs include increased interest rates, which in turn cause higher rates of default and foreclosure. These statistics cannot be viewed meaningfully on a national level; you need to study the default and foreclosure rate in your local area to spot an emerging trend.

The Rental Market

The third submarket is the *rental market*. To anyone outside of the real estate industry, it may seem surprising that rental property has different risk factors from owner-occupied property. In fact, rental rates and trends in vacancy are very revealing. If rental properties are overbuilt in a region, higher vacancy rates indicate that the rental market could experience a bubble. Real estate bubbles may easily affect multi-unit rental properties such as apartment buildings, and value would then fall because of the way that income property is appraised. The *income method* of appraisal sets market value based on net rents. So if overbuilding softens market demand, market rates fall. In addition, high vacancy rates reduce the net income from buildings, further weakening market value for those properties.

Some analysts attempt to define the value of rental properties using maximum potential rent, or rents that will be earned if a property is fully rented. But if a 20-unit building has average vacancies of three units, it means that 15 percent of maximum rent is not being earned. Logically, net market value has to be reduced by recent vacancy rates. To the extent that potential maximum rents are used to establish rental property values, the calculation creates an income property bubble.

A study of *actual* rental receipts is more realistic and more accurate. This also indicates any artificial inflation in income property values. Some income property owners will raise rents just before placing properties on the market. If the current higher rents are used to set value, it will be inflated. So to get an accurate estimate of property value, an appraiser should use actual rental income net of vacancies over the past year, and not the current rates being charged to tenants.

Chapter 8 analyzes various methods for getting into real estate beyond the three best-known equity methods (home ownership, investment, and speculation).

NOTES

1. U.S. Census Bureau, Housing Vacancy Survey and Current Population Survey, through 2005.

2. Viewed as a percentage of loan guarantees, equity value of Fannie Mae is only 1.5 percent, Ginnie Mae is 1.3 percent, and Freddie Mac is 2.4 percent, as of latest available quarterly and annual reports.

3. Marie-Christine Adam and Ariane Szafarz, "Speculative Bubbles and Financial Markets," *Oxford Economic Papers*, October 1992.

4. Hersh Shefrin, *Greed and Fear: Understanding Behavioral Finance and the Psychology of Investing* (London: Oxford University Press, 2002).

5. Federal Reserve Board, *Flow of Funds Reports*.

How to Profit in Up-and-Down Real Estate Markets

M ost people view real estate from a homeowner's perspective. The "American Dream" of home ownership is based on the idea that you buy a home, spend thirty years paying on the mortgage, and sell that home upon retirement. If you're lucky, you make a profit to augment your retirement savings.

Reality is far different. The typical first-time home buyer lives in that home for less than five years before selling. Since the mid-1970s, when the real estate secondary market was created, the widespread availability of financing makes the older view of home ownership obsolete. Few first-time buyers wait for 30 years before selling, and today's homeowners—like investors and speculators—expect their money to double within five years or less. In many markets, these expectations have been met because of bubbles and, to some extent, expansion of real demand.

That real demand often is a factor of financing itself. Without the limitations on funds that commercial lenders used to live with, risk selection is no longer a factor in granting mortgage loans. This is true because:

1. Lenders do not have to commit their own reserves to back loans on their books.

2. Loans are normally transferred to the secondary market, making traditional lenders little more than loan servicing agencies.

3. Lower interest rates have vastly expanded the pool of qualified first-time home buyers.

The very fact that lenders do not analyze risks is startling, when you consider the bigger picture of investment safety. Lenders are only concerned with qualification. So when a borrower's income is high enough to meet the required ratios of mortgage payments vs. net take-home pay, the loan can be placed into a mortgage pool or is qualified for a loan guarantee. Lenders appraise properties, but they rarely if ever ask whether a particular property is a "good risk" or a "poor risk" over the long term.

With the vast amount of mortgage obligation held by the secondary market, any widespread bubble poses a threat. If that bubble were to burst, the loan guarantees may have to be honored as growing numbers of defaulted loans end up in foreclosure. The lender originating the loan would not necessarily be stuck with a portfolio of foreclosed properties (although their contracts may require those lenders to manage the reselling of properties). The actual obligation would rest with the agency granting the loan guarantee.

While all real estate is regional, from an investment perspective there is a market-wide bubble of sorts. It may consist of some price bubbles, especially in those areas where market values have risen the most dramatically. As interest rates rise, however, first-time buyers who marginally qualified for loans are also more likely to go into default. Because higher interest rates translate to higher mortgage payments, the entire market depends on Federal Reserve policies. If rates rise too quickly, the change could lead to a real estate recession.

The obvious disparities between overall inflation and growth in housing prices indicate where the likely real estate bubbles exist. Cities where growth has exceeded 50 percent in a five-year period include San Francisco, San Diego, Boston, New York, and Minneapolis. And several of the fastest-growing areas reported 2006 *median* sales prices of homes above a half million dollars. The five areas with the highest median home sales prices as of 2006 were San Jose, California ($747,000), San Francisco ($720,000), Anaheim, California ($713,000), San Diego ($607,000), and White Plains, New York ($529,000).

This makes those high-priced, fastest-growing regions the most vulnerable to downward adjustment. Having this information helps you to make the most of any likely bubbles. The most obvious reaction, of course, is to not invest in those areas where prices have already risen dramatically. But there are other ways to strategically plan for the bubble economy, and even to earn profits when real estate values fall.

USING REAL ESTATE OPTIONS TO AVOID BIG LOSSES

The dilemma faced by every speculator is the fact that you cannot know exactly when a bubble is going to burst. If you want to make money as a speculator, but you don't want to be the "greater fool" when the bubble bursts, you face a conflict. You want to make double-digit returns, but you can't afford to lose.

There is a solution. Using *options* allows you to control real estate. When you buy an option you have the right to actually take title to property, but you are not obligated to close the deal. This means that if a bubble is on-going, you can buy an option today and exercise that option if the value continues to rise. However, if value falls, you can walk away from the deal and let the option expire. Depending on the cost of the option, this allows you to position yourself to make good money without having to place a large amount of capital at risk. For example, a $200,000 investment property might be available to buy with a $40,000 down payment. But you may be able to buy an option for only $2,000. This is not necessarily "typical" but it makes the point that an option is always going to contain far less risk than actually purchasing the property.

Options are often tied to a formal rental agreement. So if you buy a *lease option* from the current owner, your contract contains two parts: You lease the property and pay monthly rent, and you also buy an option at the same time. The term may be any number of months you both agree to. For example, you may sign a three-year lease option on a single-family home currently worth $200,000. The terms include monthly rent of $1,500 plus another $300 per month for the option, which allows you to buy the property for $225,000 before expiration. You may exercise the option any time you want up to the end of the three years, when the contract expires. At that point you no longer have to make rental payments, and your option ceases to exist.

It is likely that you either live in the property and make the rental/option payments of $1,800 yourself, or that you rent out the property to someone else, collecting rent and then paying the current owner.

Possible Outcomes

Whether you live in the property yourself or rent it out, a number of things can happen within the three-year period, including:

1. *The property value does not rise above $225,000, or it falls.* The option is set at $225,000. This means that by holding the option, you have a contractual right to buy the property at that amount. If the property value remains below $225,000, or if its market value falls, you would not exercise the option. Unless

you want to extend the lease option, the deal expires at the end of three years. You would be out the lease payments plus the option payments (minus rents you received or minus the value of living in the property for the lease term).

2. *The lease option is renegotiated under new terms.* A second possible outcome would be for you to extend both the lease and the option. Because the original lease expires after three years, either side is free to negotiate new terms. The owner may want to increase the lease payments, the option payments, or both. The owner might also want to increase the purchase price. You may prefer to keep the exercise price at the same level.

When you and the owner agree to the original lease, it makes sense to include in the contract the conditions for renegotiation. For example, if you maintain the right to renew the lease option for a higher price, but at the same purchase price upon exercise, you can include this condition in the contract. The longer you can commit the owner to a fixed exercise price for the option, the more valuable that option is to you. As property values increase you stand to gain more, and having more time for that to occur adds more flexibility to the option.

3. *The property value rises and you purchase the property.* If the property value rises above $225,000 (enough to cover closing costs and still produce a net profit), you may exercise the option. This must occur before the expiration date, because after the term expires the option is worthless.

4. *The property value rises and you sell the option.* As the property value rises, the option also grows in value. If after one year you have paid $3,600 for a three-year option (averaging out to $100 per month over the three years) and the value of the property has risen from $225,000 to $300,000, the reason for this becomes clear. The $75,000 in higher property value makes the $3,600 option more valuable as well. You may be able to sell the option back to the owner for a value greater than your actual

cost, but less than the full appreciation of the property, for example. You may also sell the option to someone else.

5. *The property value rises and you sell the property.* The most creative way to exercise the real estate option is to sell the property without taking an equity position yourself. How can you sell something you don't own? The option grants you the right to find a buyer and exercise the option as part of the same transaction, flipping the property. For example, if your option grants you the right to buy at $225,000 but current market value is $300,000, you can make a profit on the difference by selling the property.

A single closing involves a three-part process: (a) The current owner is required to relinquish the property for $225,000; (b) you sell the property to your buyer for $300,000; and (c) upon closing, your profit is the difference between the owner's sale price and the buyer's purchase price. This can be 100 percent yours as long as the seller and your new buyer pay their own closing costs.

MORTGAGE LENDING

An equity position, obtained through purchase or the use of a lease option, is not the only way to invest in real estate. You can also purchase shares in a mortgage pool offered by a secondary market agency.

Mortgage Pools

The range of *mortgage-backed securities* (MBS) includes similar products with varying names depending on the secondary market agency:

1. Real Estate Mortgage Investment Conduits (REMICs) or Stripped Mortgage Backed Securities (SMBs or Strips) are marketed by Ginnie Mae. For details on the specifics

of these products, check the Government National Mortgage Association (GNMA) website: www.ginniemae.gov.

2. Mortgage Participation Certificates (PCs), REMICs, and SMBs are marketed and organized by Freddie Mac. For details, check: www.freddiemac.com.

3. REMICs and Mortgage-Backed Security (MBS) pools and SMBs are marketed by Fannie Mae. For details, check: www.fanniemae.com.

The three secondary market organizations' products are similar and may even be identical in features, even though they are given different names. There is an active and broad market in the mortgage pool arena. By buying shares of a mortgage pool, you are lending money indirectly to a range of qualified homeowners, and your investment is backed by the equity in the homes being bought.

The REMICs offered by all three agencies are large pools of mortgages sharing similar characteristics (granted on single-family homes with fixed-rate mortgages, for example), with some REMICs modified to provide flexibility in how and when payments are made to investors. Stripped securities (called SMBs or Strips) are variations of the same idea. However, the principal and interest involved in the pool of mortgages are sold to investors separately.

The mortgage pool is considered a safe way to take a debt position in real estate. The pool involves a large number of mortgages, where the borrowers have been qualified under requirements of the pool itself and the entire pool is managed professionally. However, some investors may prefer a more direct approach.

Second Mortgages

You can take up a debt position by investing capital *directly* in second mortgages. Direct lending of money is higher risk than placing funds in a mortgage pool, with the most obvious reason being the lack of diversification involved: When you lend money to an investor or homeowner, it involves a single property. However, an equally serious risk concerns the matter of priority. When a property owner finances a purchase with a first mortgage, it establishes the priority of claims for the lender. The mortgage is "first" in the sense that upon foreclosure, the first mortgage lender's debt is to be paid before any other liens. In many foreclosure situations, there is not enough equity to pay off any mortgages except the first, so lending money through a second mortgage is a higher risk.

At first glance, a second mortgage is secured by equity, just like a first mortgage. But in the event of default, you are likely to discover that enforcing collection on your debt will be very difficult. For example, what would you do if the first mortgage is paid on time, but the property owner does not make timely payments to you for a second mortgage? To collect, you would have to acquire the first mortgage from the lender and combine first and second mortgages; and there may not be enough equity to recover your full investment. It is not so easy to take over a first mortgage, either, because—assuming the lender would be willing to reassign it—you would have to be able to cash out the loan. If the first mortgage balance is $250,000 and your second mortgage is only $10,000, the attempt to acquire the entire debt might be fruitless (again assuming the mortgage holder would sell it to you, *and* assuming you have another $250,000 sitting around free and clear).

Second mortgages are attractive because the interest rate is usually considerably higher than rates for first mortgages. Some individuals accept the obvious risks by lending funds selectively. If you decide to venture into the direct lending business, you should select your borrowers with extreme care. This means obtaining and checking their credit reports, evaluating their equity in the property, and ensuring that their income is healthy enough to afford to make repayments. In other words, if you are going to lend money to someone, your process should be at least as thorough as that of a commercial lender—and probably more so.

LIMITED PARTNERSHIPS AND REITs

Some forms of "pooled" investments—in which investors place their capital with the capital of many other investors to be managed as a single, larger unit—should be considered as an alternative way of investing in the real estate market. These vehicles include limited partnerships and REITs.

Limited Partnerships

For most investors, limited partnerships are not good choices. There are several reasons for this. Up until the early 1980s investors were allowed to deduct losses in limited partnerships well in excess of the amounts they invested. In a "four-to-one" program, for example, an investor could spend $10,000 and deduct $40,000.

This abusive tax shelter practice was stopped through tax reform in 1986. But before that happened, limited partnerships were highly popular. They enabled many wealthy people to completely avoid taxes on their income. Today, limited partnerships still exist, but there are few arguments supporting the idea of investing in them. Consider these points:

1. *No Tax Benefits.* You cannot deduct losses from limited partnerships, which are classified as "passive" activity. That term applies to any investment in which you have no direct management or control. So losses have to be carried forward and applied against future passive gains. The old-style multiple write-off of losses is no longer allowed. Even when you have deductible passive gains, you are limited to only the amount you have "at risk," which means you cannot deduct more than the amount you invest or obligate yourself to in such programs.

2. *Spotty Record of Profits.* Most limited partnerships cannot point to spectacular net profits for their investors. The general partners—the people who organize these programs—compensate themselves handsomely, but many people who have bought units in limited partnerships see little profit, if any.

3. *No Secondary Market.* You will hear that you can resell your limited partnership units. But there is no auction market-place. The resell of units takes place only at a deep discount. Because you will definitely lose a lot of money in order to escape from limited partnerships, there is no real secondary market.

4. *No Liquidity.* The lack of a secondary market, coupled with historical low cash flow (if any), means that investing in limited partnerships provides you with no liquidity. Your funds are going to be committed for many years and they may end up worthless. If and when you receive any funds back, that occurs only well in the future.

REITs

A possible solution to the many problems of limited partnerships is the Real Estate Investment Trust (REIT). The collective invest-ments of many shareholders are combined together to purchase and invest in real estate. But unlike the poor liquidity of limited partnerships, REIT shares are traded over public exchanges just like stocks. For this reason, REITs are often referred to as "real estate stocks." This is not entirely accurate because a REIT is not exactly like a stock, but your ability to invest small amounts and to buy and sell shares cheaply and quickly makes REITs a popular alternative to other pooled investment alternatives.

Most REIT programs identify the kinds of properties manage-ment will purchase; some even list specific properties before they sell shares. Typically, REITs specialize. So one type of REIT might be designed to purchase and operate shopping centers, and another industrial/office parks. There are as many kinds of

REITS as there are investors, so picking the REIT most appropriate for how you want to invest is not difficult.

The REIT is an efficient and affordable way for you to invest part of your capital in commercial real estate. Few people can afford to build a shopping center or industrial park, but buying shares of a REIT that does so (and manages the property professionally) is as easy as buying shares of stock.

REITs come in many defined forms, including:

1. *Equity REITs*. The safest and most traditional form is the equity REIT. This program buys and manages properties, often with absolutely no debt whatsoever. Management enters into leases and collects rents, maintains properties, reports to shareholders, and sends out distributions of profits each quarter.

2. *Mortgage REITs*. The mortgage REIT lends money to others to build projects or invest in mortgages directly. One variation is called the *construction* REIT, designed to finance the building of large projects. Builders and developers are the most likely borrowers of funds. The risk of construction REITs is that property values may change or construction costs may run higher than originally estimated, meaning the project may not be completed for the amount financed. Some mortgage REITs are less risky, specializing in offering secured debts on existing properties.

3. *Hybrid REITs*. The hybrid REIT combines both equity and debt in its investment portfolio. Any investor should know in advance what the REIT's policies and limitations are for portions of total assets to be invested in each.

EXCHANGE TRADED FUNDS

Besides partnerships and REITs, you can also invest in real estate through the purchase of mutual fund shares. A relatively new kind of mutual fund is the Exchange Traded Fund (ETF).

This is different from traditional funds in several ways, and these distinctions are important. They include:

1. *Purchase and sale of shares takes place on the exchange.* The traditional mutual fund requires investors to buy or sell shares directly with the fund management. This is cumbersome and time-consuming. The ETF, by comparison, can be bought and sold over the public exchanges as quickly as it takes to place an order. Thus, anyone with an online discount brokerage account can trade ETF funds in the same way he trades stocks. This is a huge convenience and has revolutionized the mutual fund industry.

2. *The ETF portfolio is identified in advance as a "basket of stocks."* Under old-style fund policies, a fund was identified and distinguished only by way of broadly stated goals, like "conservative growth," "aggressive growth," or "income." But these definitions did not really tell investors exactly which stocks the fund management would buy or sell. In fact, management in traditional funds changes its portfolio often, adding new stocks and selling old ones. So investors have no way of knowing beforehand the mix of a portfolio.

In the ETF, the fund itself is identified by the "components" in its portfolio. This "basket of stocks" consists of specific types (such as a single market sector in a country, or a product such as real estate). In determining how to diversify investment assets among different types of markets, ETFs offer a better alternative than traditional mutual funds because of this concentration.

3. *Management fees are much lower than for traditional mutual funds.* Because the components (stocks) are identified in advance, portfolio management is virtually automatic. Thus, management fees and expenses are minimal in comparison to traditional mutual funds. For example, one study concluded that typical expense ratios for actively managed (traditional) funds have been rising over the past two to three decades and today

average 1.4 percent (with some over 2 percent) of total assets. In comparison, most ETFs charge at least a full percentage point less than the managed fund average.

4. *ETFs allow the trading of options.* For investors who understand options, ETFs offer one additional form of flexibility. Options (not to be confused with real estate lease options explained earlier in this chapter) allow investors to speculate on share prices of ETFs without actually having to buy or sell shares. Options are available on many listed stocks, and including ETFs in this classification makes them incredibly flexible for a much larger cross-section of investors. For example, options are traded on all four of the major real estate ETFs, listed below:

iShares Cohen and Steers Realty Majors Fund
    Traded as ICF, this ETF has about 30 components
    Expense ratio: 0.35 percent
street TRACKS Wilshire REIT Fund
    Traded as RWR, it has about 90 stocks in its portfolio
    Expense ratio: 0.26 percent
iShares Dow Jones US Real Estate Index
    Traded as IYR, this ETF has about 85 stocks
    Expense ratio: 0.60 percent
Vanguard REIT VIPER
    Traded as VNQ, it has over 100 stocks
    Expense ratio: 0.12 percent[2]

The ETF is not only a major departure from the traditional mutual fund format, it is also an entirely new product, unlike mutual funds in many respects. Before ETFs were introduced, investors desiring investment in real estate through any pooled accounts needed to buy shares in REITs or limited partnerships, or to buy publicly listed shares in companies that own and manage real estate directly. Although all of these alternatives exist, none are as convenient as the ETF.

Given the potential for loss of money through direct ownership of real estate in a bubble environment, the ETF alternative provides a measure of safety in many respects. If the bubble is focused on residential property, you can purchase ETF shares that concentrate on commercial real estate or in a diversified portfolio. Since many real estate ETFs invest in a basket of REIT shares, you also achieve "double diversification" as well as multi-layered professional management. This protects your investment assets from the immediate problems of market value declines if and when bubbles burst.

When you compare direct ownership of residential property to diversified purchase of ETF shares (and their own diversification among dozens of REIT shares), the decision to buy ETF shares provides you with much greater safety and protection. ETF investment is liquid and enables you to spread a limited amount of capital around into many different markets.

STOCK OPTIONS ON REAL ESTATE

A final way to augment potential profits from real estate is through the use of listed stock options, which are entirely different from real estate lease options. A listed stock option is an intangible contract you can buy against stock. These are complex financial products that should only be used by experienced investors who thoroughly understand the risks and mechanics of investing. To read about the range of risks in this market, check the web page for the Options Clearing Corporation (OCC) at www.optionsclearing.com and download the free booklet, "Characteristics and Risks of Standardized Options."

Options are interesting because they can be used to create profits when stocks go up *and* when stocks go down. So options can be written on stocks as well as on real estate ETFs. Following is a brief overview of how options work:

1. *Types of Options.* The option is intangible. Stock grants you a specific value as part of a corporation, and real estate own-

ership includes the land and improvements. But options are merely contracts without any physical value. There are two types of options: calls and puts.

Buying a *call* gives you the right (but not the obligation) to buy, say, 100 shares of a specific, named stock (called the "underlying security"). You pay a price for this option, which is called the premium. If you exercise the call, you can buy 100 shares of stock at a fixed price (called the "strike price" of the option) even if the current market value is much higher.

The second type of option is the *put*. If you buy a put, you have the right (but again, not the obligation) to sell 100 shares of stock. So even if market value is much lower than the put's strike price, you still get that price by exercising the put option.

2. *Expiration Term.* Every option expires on a specific date in the future. Most options expire within eight months, but long-term options can last up to three years. Once the expiration date is reached, all options become worthless immediately. So before an option expires, its owner must take one of three steps. First, if the underlying stock's value has risen, you can exercise the option and buy 100 shares below current market value. Second, you can sell the call at a profit. Third, if the underlying stock is worth less than the call's strike price, you take no action and allow it to expire.

3. *Fixed Purchase or Sale Prices.* The most important feature to both calls and puts is that the strike price is fixed. This is specific with each and every option. Anyone who buys a call hopes the underlying stock's value will rise; it makes the option more valuable, whether it is sold at a profit or exercised. And the opposite is true of a put. When you own a put, you make a profit if the underlying security's market value falls.

4. *Cost and Value of Options.* The premium you pay for an option is going to be based on several important attributes. First is the proximity between the current market value of stock and the strike price of the option. Second is whether the current mar-

ket value is higher than a call or lower than a put. When this occurs, the option is "in the money" and its value will rise or fall point-for-point with changes in the underlying stock's price. Third is the amount of time remaining until expiration. The more time left, the more valuable the option. This time feature is called *time value* and for options with a very long time to go, it can be most or even all of the premium value.

5. *Buying Options.* Typically, people start out in the options market by speculating on short-term price changes of stock. They buy calls or puts hoping that enough points will change in market value to make their option more valuable. For example, if a stock is now worth $37.50 per share and you buy a 40 call (the strike price is $40 per share) expiring next May, you might pay $300. This grants you the right to buy 100 shares of the stock at $40 per share, even if the actual market value moves much higher. The cost of an option also depends on how long a time there is until expiration. All options expire at the close of the third Friday of the indicated expiration month. In option shorthand, this would be called a May 40 call at 3, or a call expiring on the third Friday in May, at a cost of $300. If the stock rises above $40 per share, the call will become more valuable; if the stock remains below $40, the time value will evaporate as May approaches.

Now consider what happens if instead of buying a 40 call, you buy a May 35 put and pay $250. This would be described as a May 35 put at 2.50. If the stock's value falls below $35 per share before the third Friday in May, the put will increase in value; but if the stock's market value remains at or above $35, the put will expire worthless.

6. *Selling Options on Stock You Own.* A very profitable way to trade options is to *sell* them instead of buying them. About three out of every four options expire worthless, so buying options is highly speculative. In comparison, if you sell an option, you have a better chance of making a profit. For many people,

the concept of selling something as a first step and then buying it later is confusing. Investors are used to the sequence of buy-hold-sell and are less familiar with the opposite, sell-hold-buy. But it is perfectly legal.

A conservative way to do this is to sell a call against 100 shares of stock that you own. In this way, if the call is exercised (meaning your stock is "called away"), you have the stock available to deliver. You get to keep the option premium because, when you sell an option, you are paid instead of the other way around. So to calculate a profit, you should ensure that the strike price of the option is higher than the price per share you paid for the stock. In that case, if the call is exercised, you will have three types of profit: capital gains on the stock, a profit on the call, and dividends.

Selling a call against 100 shares you own is a strategy called a "covered call." You cannot actually cover a put, so there is no corresponding strategy on the other side.

7. *Selling Options on Stock You Do Not Own.* A relatively high-risk strategy is selling calls when you do not own the underlying stock. If the market value of the stock rises before expiration, you would have to deliver 100 shares at the fixed strike price, which could be considerably lower than market value. Your loss in this situation would be the difference in price between market value at the time of exercise, and the strike price, minus the call premium you received. For example, if you sell a May 40 call and receive 3 ($300), and the stock later rises to $48 per share, exercise would create a net loss of $500 ($4,800 market value, less $4,000 strike price = $800 loss on the stock, less $300 call premium earned = net loss of $500).

Selling a put is somewhat less risky than selling a call, but both strategies are called "uncovered" or "naked" because no shares are owned. If you sell a put and the stock's market value falls, you would be required to buy 100 shares at the strike price. So the stock would be "put to you" at a price above current market value. For example, if you sell a May 35 put and you receive premium of 2.50 ($250), and the put is exercised when the stock is valued at $29 per share, your loss would be $350 ($3,500 strike price less $2,900 market value of stock = $600 loss, less $250 received from put premium = net loss of $350).

Using Options with Real Estate

It takes a while to absorb all of the nuances and master the terminology of the options market. But this is an important strategy for long-term investing in real estate. For example, if you buy shares of a real estate ETF or a company in the real estate industry, how can you protect your equity position if a bubble bursts? There are several ways to achieve this protection using options, including:

1. *Buying Puts to Speculate.* If you do not own stock but you expect real estate values to fall dramatically, it is also reasonable to expect share value of real estate stocks to fall. If you buy puts and speculate on this occurring before the puts expire, you will profit if your timing is correct.

2. *Buying Puts for Insurance.* If you own shares in a real estate ETF or a real estate management company, and you are concerned about the bubble, you can buy puts as a form of insurance, holding one put per 100 shares you own. Thus, if the share value of your stock does fall, the puts will increase one dollar for each point lost in the stock. So any losses will be offset by your put insurance.

3. *Selling Covered Calls to Reduce Your Basis.* Ownership of real estate shares can be protected by selling covered calls. This reduces your basis in the stock. For example, if you buy shares at $37.50 and sell calls receiving $300 in premium, your net basis in those shares is reduced to $34.50. This provides you with downside protection, because your net basis is reduced below the stock's current market value.

This brief overview of options is intended only to demonstrate that there are many ways to protect your equity positions in real estate, or to speculate in the market without owning property directly. If you are concerned about real estate bubbles, the options market and the many strategies available can produce profits in all types of markets, even those markets where property values are falling.

Chapter 9 explores market profitability from another angle: What can you do *after* the bubble bursts. Figuring out how to time your real estate decisions—and avoiding the emotions of greed and fear—can help you to become an expert in profiting after the bubble has burst.

NOTES

1. National Association of Realtors.
2. Carol A. Wood, "Real Estate Plays, Hassle-Free," *Business Week Online*, July 21, 2005.

How to Profit
When the Bubble Pops

What goes up must come down. However, most discussion focuses on markets on the way up. It is "news" when prices rise and people make easy money in a short period of time. But it is not news when the market goes into recession. In fact, anyone who reads or listens to the financial news realizes that the audience loses interest unless prices are going up.

This presents a problem for the serious investor. How do you judge the market when news sources simply dry up? First off, you should recognize that the common financial news is not news at all, but pop culture. The shallow coverage you see on television or read in most newspapers is useless for making informed decisions. Financial news often consists primarily in (1) predicting the Dow Jones Industrial Averages for the coming weeks or months (which, like predicting the weather, is mainly guesswork); (2) recommending specific stocks (in spite of the probability that risk levels vary among different issues and no one stock is appropriate for everyone); and (3) making alarming non-specific warnings about the future (such as an eventual tumble in stock prices, a coming nationwide real estate depression, or a new round of corporate scandals on the horizon).

These popular financial news stories are repeated continually, but they are of little value to the serious investors, who need fundamental information. In the stock market, this data is considered dry and uninteresting, but serious investors do need to track revenues and earnings, apply tests to track trends in capitalization and profitability, and ensure the safety of their investments. In real estate, the fundamentals are local and, unlike with stocks, you should be focused on what is taking place where you live. Indicators like the current inventory of homes for sale, the spread, and time on the market are far more revealing and useful than listening to someone in a television studio in New York predicting that the bottom is about to fall out of real estate.

BUYING DEPRESSED REAL ESTATE

Remembering that all real estate is local, it is a safe policy to ignore what you read and hear in the financial news, with the exception of the rare thoughtful article or story. If you track real estate trends locally, you will gain a sense of how the market is changing, you will begin to recognize trends, and you will become an expert in timing your decisions to buy and sell within your local market.

Not every real estate cycle consists of a rapidly expanding bubble, followed by a deep recession. That is the exception to the rule. It is far more likely that the cycle will lead to price growth in the real estate market. So it is possible to track the fundamental trends in real estate and identify buying or selling opportunities. You will also be able to identify the time to stay out of the market. The problem, of course, is in making these determinations in a timely manner, or developing foresight that is as astute as hindsight.

Every real estate cycle has a unique rhythm to it. This does not mean you can time decisions perfectly. It is the very uncertainty about cyclical movement that makes timing most difficult. But you will begin to recognize repetitive tendencies. For example, in some regions, a rise in prices and fundamental strength may grow over approximately three years, followed by a gradual slow-down lasting about two years. In another market, the cycle might be much shorter or longer. Once you have identified the usual length of a cyclical direction, you will be better equipped to time your decisions. Your educated guess is preferable to making decisions without any awareness of the cycle's timing.

When real estate prices are rising rapidly, you can speculate on the trend without risking great sums of money. For example, you can purchase options from current owners, knowing that you might lose the money placed into the option, but also knowing that this is preferable to actually buying property only to lose a larger sum of money. With an option in hand, you can find a buyer, go into escrow, and complete a buy-and-sell at the same time without risking any equity. This works when market prices are rising, but you would be smart to identify the point where you will need to exit from the position. For example, you might identify a percentage or net dollar amount. Without an exit strategy, it is far too easy to give in to greed, wait too long, and miss the opportunity.

When prices have fallen, people tend to rely on their fear. They become desperate to sell, thinking that prices will continue downward. By keeping a cool head, you can find real bargains at such times. When it is a buyer's market, you can demand and get deep discounts from asked prices and acquire real estate below market value. Remember, even when people are fearful about real estate trends, falling prices (or, more likely, flattening out of a rising trend) are usually a temporary situation, even as a follow-up in some real estate bubbles. The actual precipitous drop in prices is rare. However, when that does occur, it presents an ever bigger opportunity for the buyer who is able to keep a cool head.

There are three primary strategies in a buyer's market. These are:

1. Invest in rental property long term or intermediate term.

2. Buy property with depressed price *and* depressed condition as a fixer-upper strategy.

3. Flip properties using one of several techniques.

Buying Rental Properties

When prices are down you can find bargains; when prices are flat, current owners are often fearful. The tendency is to believe that when price increases stop, the trend will never turn around. Despair, grown from fear, motivates people to sell their properties for less than they are worth.

When you buy rental property, the immediate goal is to create a situation in which rent income is high enough to make your mortgage payment and to cover all expenses. You are less likely to have vacancies when the rental market remains strong. Even when housing prices fall or go flat, the rental demand market is separate and may remain strong. This is a good time to get into the business of holding property as investment, covering expenses through rents, and waiting for prices to return to the upside.

There are two ways to enter the investment market in housing. The first and most obvious way is to purchase property through conventional methods. The higher your down payment, the lower your monthly mortgage obligation and the easier it will be to make positive cash flow. But at the same time, the more capital you tie up in a single property, the more opportunities you have to pass on, and the higher your risks. Buying rental property is a dilemma because you need to balance the requirement of positive cash flow against the desirability of leveraging your capital.

An alternative method—and one that makes a lot of sense when the local market is depressed—is using the *lease option* (see Chapter 8). When current owners are in despair because prices have fallen, they are far more likely to accept an offer of a lease option contract—because they do not believe they are going to be able to sell the property for a high price. The psychology of any investor or property owner is most likely to operate on the basis of greed (on the way up) and fear (on the way down). At the market bottom, an offer of a lease option solves many problems for a property owner:

- First, it creates an income stream.

- Second, it removes the current owner from the direct contact with tenants or continued payment of mortgage without income (your payments to the owner will cover the payments).

- Third, it creates a potential purchase in the future, perhaps at an amount higher than today's market value.

If your timing is off and property values remain flat or do not rise, your lease option is a limited potential loss. And if you rent out the property to a tenant, your cost is covered as well. If the market value does rise before the option runs out, you can sell the property through the option, and walk away with your profit.

The rental market can be odd, and many people forget to make the distinction between home prices (of which the majority are for owner-occupied homes) and rental demand. These distinctly different markets operate on dissimilar cycles. Within the rental market, there are at least two strata of general demand. The most common is the apartment market, which caters to younger people, newlyweds, students, or those with low-paying jobs.

Another submarket consists of people who can afford to pay somewhat more rent than the typical apartment market, and who want to live in a house. This may be a married couple wanting to start a family or with one or two children, who are attracted to the features of home ownership like tending a garden or owning a small pet, and who view living in a house as a form of social status. This market tends to remain strong even when excess apartment units are available. The rental *housing* market—meaning houses rather than apartments—often is a low-vacancy market even when the overall rental market reports higher or growing vacancy rates. So even if the market has slowed down in the post-bubble, you may be able to employ property flipping with single-family housing, although you may have to extend the process over a longer period.

You may also speculate in bargain-priced properties using a combination of lease option contracts and rentals. With a lease option, you can find a tenant and set rents to cover all or most of your payment costs. If the property value increases beyond the option price during the lease period, you can sell the property by exercising the option, and make your profit without risking capital. With an option, you can profit from a renewed upward cycle, but without investing a down payment in the property.

Buying Fixer-Uppers

In addition to buying and holding rental property or speculating in real estate, another method is to buy property, fix it up, and sell it. This is not necessarily the same as flipping property. A property flip involves exceptionally fast turnaround, with a sale arranged in some cases before the purchase is even completed. The fixer-upper investor, on the other hand, may hold onto property for several months and even put tenants in place for up to a year or more. This fixer-upper market is widespread and popular. For those who know how to identify the attributes of the right property, this can be a lucrative market. Here are several things to consider in this type of situation:

• *The property should be in poor condition, but only cosmetically.* An old adage in real estate recommends you "buy the worst house on a good block." This is sound advice, especially when you remember that a run-down house is likely to appreciate to the average values of properties nearby. So the best fixer-upper candidate is a run-down property on a block where other homes look much better, are manicured and taken care of, and hold their value reasonably well. When prices flatten out or fall after a bubble, well-cared-for homes will hold value better than ones that have been neglected; this means the property is likely to be sold at a bargain price.

• *You will be able to own the property for as short a time as possible.* You will profit best when you own a fixer-upper for as short a time as possible. The longer you have to own the property, the more you have to pay to a lender, as well as in insurance, property taxes, and utilities. So your incentive should be to make repairs as quickly as possible and put the property back on the market.

This is not always easy. You have to own the property to make repairs, and so you have to wait for the sale to close. You then need to fix the obvious problems before you can list the property; otherwise, you won't get the maximum profit. So you will need to hold the property for a period of time, and the expense of this has to be factored into your estimates of how much profit you can expect.

• *To maximize profits, you may consider living in the property while you complete repairs.* Some people simply cannot move frequently or live in a home that is under repair. The stress can ruin marriages, disrupt routines, and make any potential profit not worth the trouble. But a young couple without children, wanting to work together and build some equity, can certainly move from one fixer-upper to another. One big advantage of living in the property is that the cost of the mortgage and utilities is something you'd have to pay anyhow, which gives you greater flexibility in how long to hold onto the property. Living in the house makes perfect sense, assuming that you are able to deal with the chaos and stress of doing repairs where you live.

Another alternative is to rent out the property while you are doing the repairs. This raises potential problems. You don't have complete and free access once you give possession to tenants, and trying to do repairs when they are living in the house can become a problem, even if a tenant agrees to let you do the work.

   • *Repairs should be inexpensive and primarily cosmetic.* The most important aspect of fixer-upper work is that you have to be able to afford the repairs and pay out as little as possible to other people. A common problem is underestimating the cost of the repairs and finding out once you get into the investment that what really needs to be done to resell the house at a certain price may eat up most of what you hoped to profit. The ideal types of repairs are those that you can perform yourself, preferably with a minimum of material costs. If you are a skilled carpenter or plumber, you have an advantage.

   The repairs most likely to fit the description of "cosmetic" are landscaping, inside and outside painting, and minor inside repairs. The so-called lipstick approach to fixer-upper repairs may or may not produce profits. It all depends on how long you can afford to hold the property, how values are changing in the neighborhood, and whether prices are inflated or depressed. The viability of fixer-upper strategies depends on a complete analysis of your local market as well as a clear idea about what repairs actually cost. The best fixer-upper is a house with a depressed price and a depressed condition, located in a neighborhood where prices have been generally stable or rising.

Property-Flipping Strategies

One of the most effective techniques for profiting from real estate while bubbles are growing is flipping. This involves buying property (or controlling property via options) and then selling at a profit. This may occur quite rapidly. For example, some people act as go-between, setting up sellers and buyers and taking a profit in the middle by arranging a three-way closing. That kind of flip involves zero days of ownership and, while extreme, is typical of the ideal property-flipping environment. A property flipper may also find a new buyer immediately upon closing (or even before close) and hold title to the property for only a matter of weeks, even days.

Property flippers often execute a complete buy-and-sell in a very short time, often using one escrow process, acting as scouts for other speculators, or holding properties for a very short time only. The challenge with property flipping in a bubble environment is knowing when to get out. The tendency when short-term profits have been earned is to roll funds into more property, increasing the amount of capital at risk and seeking even higher profits. If the "greed factor" controls property-flipping decisions, the speculator often loses everything.

After a bubble has burst or when prices level out, property-flipping strategies can still be executed but with a different emphasis. Assuming that property values fall after a bubble, current owners may panic and sell their properties quickly. Fearing further declines, bargain pricing may follow and, even when sellers advertise a specific price, they might come down even more. Because a post-bubble economy is dominated by fear, buyers can find many discounts on the market. The secret is to recognize that fear, like greed, is irrational, and to avoid responding to these emotions. Cool-headed investors can profit in all types of market conditions.

Post-bubble conditions are going to be characterized by an excess of properties on the market. This can make flipping less practical than in conditions when prices are driven higher by an excess of buyers. Even so, those likely bargain prices present an opportunity. Your property-flipping strategy may need to be extended beyond the short-term approach.

You can seek depressed fixer-upper properties and try to re-sell, but in a soft market it is unlikely that you will be able to make the profit you would earn in a stronger market. The most likely alternative when prices are depressed is to pick up bargain-priced properties and rent them out. If you can cover your payments and expenses through rent, this is a perfect strategy for waiting out the post-bubble cycle. It is especially practical when you face the common disparity in demand levels between market prices and rentals.

MOVING YOUR CAPITAL TO OTHER MARKETS

You may find news of the real estate market stressful, notably when so many people are predicting bubble recessions. With the uncertainty of the real estate market prevalent in the minds of investors and homeowners, two suggestions are worth considering.

First, if you believe you paid a fair price for your home and you can afford the payments, separate that property from all investment considerations. Remember, your home represents more for your family than profits, and your judgment about your home should not be clouded by the profit motive.

Second, if you share the apprehension of so many people in the real estate market, allocate more of your investment capital to other markets, and less in directly owned property. This means moving out of real estate *or* moving funds from individual properties and into pooled programs.

The two markets worth considering outside of real estate are stocks (direct ownership or mutual fund shares) and the money market. Most people will not speculate beyond these markets, as they represent a broad range of investment possibilities.

1. *Stocks.* You can participate in the stock market by investing in shares of individual companies, or by buying shares of mutual funds. Many types of funds are available and can suit your risk tolerance and personal investing profile, defined by degrees of risk or by product type. An "aggressive" fund aims at earning greater profits but also is higher risk. A "conservative" fund is more suitable for anyone who is willing to accept lower profits in exchange for less risk. Funds can also be distinguished by the type of investments they make. An equity fund concentrates on

stocks; an income fund includes stocks paying higher than average dividends, and bonds yielding attractive interest rates; and a balanced fund combines investments in both stocks and bonds.

2. *The Money Market.* The broad "debt" market is also called the money market. Anyone who lends money to someone else has invested in the money market. It includes buying bonds (or shares in an income or bond mutual fund), personal savings accounts, certificates of deposit, and money market funds or accounts.

Asset Allocation

You have numerous choices of where and how to invest. You are not limited to purchasing property directly, or in being involved with real estate at all. The practice of asset allocation (in which you make a conscious choice of how much to invest in each market) is not a precise science. In fact, it often focuses only on investment assets and overlooks the importance of your personal residence. While it is not wise to use your property as an investment asset (for example, selling because you think prices have moved too high), the value of your investment should be taken into account within an asset allocation program. For example, consider the following analysis:

Total investment assets:		$320,000
Asset allocation:		
Stocks	50%	$160,000
Real estate ETFs	25%	$ 80,000
Money market	25%	$ 80,000

Now review the same analysis including your personal residence, based on its assumed total value of $450,000 minus current mortgage of $250,000 (so that your net equity value is $200,000):

Total investment assets (including personal residence):		$520,000
Asset allocation:		
Stocks	31%	$160,000
Real estate	54%	$280,000
(including residence)		
Money market	15%	$ 80,000

This realignment of the allocation percentages changes everything. If you had entered into a conscious plan to allocate 50-25-25, you would position investments to achieve that outcome. But including your home equity, you end up with a 31-54-15 allocation. This might be entirely unacceptable based on your preconceived desire to have a 50-25-25. In practice, it makes no sense to ignore your equity in your home. However, the desired allocation percentage should not mandate how you invest either. Let's say that, from this analysis, you decide you are not comfortable being 54 percent invested in real estate. You could move the non–home equity portion to the money market, which would change the breakdown to:

Total investment assets (including personal residence):		$520,000
Asset allocation:		
Stocks	31%	$160,000
Real estate	38%	$200,000
Money market	31%	$160,000

This adjustment reduces your overall exposure to real estate to 38 percent. But is it reasonable to balance stocks and money market at the same level? It might not be. Perhaps you want your stock allocation to be higher—say, $200,000 (38 percent) or $260,000 (50 percent)—in which case your money market allocation would then be $120,000 (24 percent) or $60,000 (12 percent). Conversely, if you wanted a little less risk, you might increase your money market allocation to $200,000 (38 percent) and lower your stock allocation to $120,000 (24 percent).

There are two points to be emphasized here. First, it makes sense to evaluate *all* of your assets in trying to decide how to allocate capital, including your home equity. Second, an assumed desirable split among the different markets should not be the final factor in deciding exactly how to invest funds. Asset allocation is a useful tool for risk evaluation, but you need to make your investment decisions based on logic and the desirability of various markets.

For example, how much should you invest in stocks? The question is unreasonable by itself. Within the stock market, there are endless variations and risk levels to choose from. Buying shares of mutual funds may be less risky than buying shares directly. Some market sectors are higher risk or lower risk than others. A more accurate way to decide how much to invest in stocks is to make distinctions between well-established and well-capitalized companies (Blue Chip) and initial public offerings (IPOs), between different types of equity mutual funds, and between various market sectors.

The same argument applies to real estate. A detailed allocation program would be more accurate if you were to break down "real estate" into several subgroups: your home, directly owned rental property, properties controlled through lease options, and real estate owned through shares of ETFs, REITs, or mortgage pools. All of these subgroups are dramatically different from one another in terms of risk levels, capital investment requirements, and potential income.

MAINTAINING BUBBLE PERSPECTIVES

Real estate—as an investment and in terms of any bubble situations—has to be kept in perspective. All investments are characterized by specific market activity and action, and investors behave in very specific ways. But in all markets, a few things never change. These include three important observations:

1. Greed and fear dominate investor behavior.

2. Prices never move in the same direction forever.

3. The fundamentals always disclose important information, but they are the most likely to be ignored.

Chapter 10 concludes this book with a discussion of how real estate can be incorporated into your overall financial plan to help reach your long-term investment goals.

Real Estate in
Your Portfolio

R eal estate bubbles are fueled by rapidly increasing market value. In fact, the entire discussion of real estate—as primary residence, investment, or vehicle for speculation—is centered primarily on market value. Yet you know from any detailed study of markets that price is only one of several considerations.

This applies to analysis of real estate by itself. But it is not realistic to study real estate as an investment opportunity without coordinating it with a broader picture of your personal financial plan and investment program. The specific attributes of every investment have to be merged into your plan and coordinated with each other. You need to consider the degree of capital you want in real estate (allocation) and how you spread that capital around in different products (diversification). So you also need to critically review your larger portfolio in terms of liquidity levels, risk (and your own risk tolerance), and whether or not any specific investment or strategy is even appropriate for you.

A lot of emphasis is put on analysis within the stock market, with dozens of systems in place for measuring, valuing, and anticipating stock prices. Because it is easy to track prices on a daily basis, it creates the *illusion* that the stock market is easy to follow and to understand. But the day-to-day market is chaotic and price movement is impossible to calculate, either short term or long term, because no one can really know the entire cause and effect of market pricing. Large changes in market value invariably take at least half of the market by surprise. So one conclusion you can draw is that the stock market is not as easy to understand as people think. Just because minute-to-minute market values are easy to find does not mean that the reasons for change are made clear.

This applies equally to real estate. The stock market and the real estate market operate under separate structures, but *both markets are difficult to read* in terms of how cyclical change is occurring, the direction of price trends, and even the elements of change in supply and demand. Experts and insiders know as little as anyone about the markets—both stocks and real estate—and even with favorite "yardsticks" of market behavior, they are generally right only about half the time. The separate methods of identifying value make no difference, however. Both markets operate chaotically in the short term. So any assumptions are dangerous.

Some common assumptions include unsupportable beliefs like *when the bubble bursts everyone who owns real estate will lose* and, on the other extreme, *real estate is a sure thing.* Neither of these beliefs are true, and the fundamentals in the real estate market prove it. The major difference between the stock market and the real estate market involves location. Stocks are universal because they trade everywhere, no matter where company headquarters is located. (Of course, this means that "the market" is also vulnerable everywhere.) Real estate is strictly local, so national averages are useless and the possibility of bubbles bursting elsewhere will not affect local values. (In this sense, the limited physical market for real estate protects you against national events, even within the real estate market.)

REVIEWING THE BASICS OF DIVERSIFICATION

It makes sense to evaluate real estate using realistic assumptions and applying sound investment principles. This simple suggestion is offered here because it is so often *not* how investors operate. If you study companies in great detail before buying stocks, you are performing the responsible preliminary step of determining before you buy stock whether it is well priced or not. But do you apply the same practice to real estate? If you do, you are the exception, because many people—including seasoned investors who are diligent in their fundamental analysis of stocks—are passive when it comes to real estate investment decisions.

The fundamentals—specifically the easily available information that describes the health of the real estate market in your city—include the three key tests: inventory for sale, time on the market, and the spread. You can further evaluate the fundamentals of the rental market by evaluating vacancy rates over the past year (ideally separating single-family vacancy trends from multi-unit housing vacancies). And you can easily study the fundamentals of the financing market by watching interest rate trends.

The financing aspect to the overall fundamental analysis of real estate is the only portion that is not solely regional, and this is also the most difficult to estimate. A "trend" in value or rental is easily identified, but changes in interest rates cannot be so readily pinned down. The only insulation from financing change is for those who already own property and have financed their purchase with a fixed-rate mortgage. Even then, the protection applies only to the specific property and its affordability.

Market value continues to be vulnerable to the bubble effect; when rates rise, demand falls and housing prices are likely to follow. Therefore, a study of the fundamentals has to take into account the overall risk from all three submarkets in real estate: market price, rentals, and financing.

Investors may not recognize the importance of fundamental analysis in real estate, even when they apply it diligently to stocks. An equally dangerous assumption is the belief that diversification and allocation do not apply to real estate.

What Diversification Means

Diversification is often described as "*not* putting all of your eggs in one basket." In the stock market, the most common application is the advice to not buy just one stock. This has led to widespread popularity of mutual funds, where even a small amount of money is spread out among many different stocks or bonds. But diversification should mean much more, and applying this concept to stocks reveals how important it is to apply it to real estate as well. Diversification in terms of the stock market should follow these basic rules:

1. *Avoid one sector exclusively.* The stock market is divided into specific sectors; putting all of your capital into just one sector is a mistake. It is not sufficient to buy several stocks if the companies are all in a single sector, like retail, pharmaceutical, or computer hardware. Diversification should involve dissimilar and separate sectors.

2. *Be aware that different sectors may be subject to the same cyclical forces.* In diversifying among sectors within the market, you also need to remember that some sectors—while distinct and apart from one another—are subject to the same economic cycle. So sectors that are cyclical may share a similar cycle, just as companies whose revenue and earnings vary by season may extend over more than one sector.

3. *Invest in other products as well.* No matter how well you diversify within the stock market, you are not truly diversified unless you also invest money elsewhere. This is why real estate

and the money market (savings, certificates of deposit, and money market funds, for example) are the two obvious alternatives to stocks.

4. *Diversify in terms of features of products.* Product-based diversification is essential to a well-managed portfolio. But equally important is the question of how you diversify by features of the product. Most important among these are *market risk* and *liquidity*. Your capital should not be invested in products that have the same level of market risk. And although virtually everyone needs some liquidity (availability of funds) in case of emergency, you should not put an entire portfolio into all-liquid investments. An equally important definition of liquidity refers to one's ability to sell the product. Stocks have a tremendous liquidity level because the public exchanges always will buy your shares for the current prices. On the opposite extreme, limited partnership shares have no real secondary market. There are places to sell units, but only at deep discount.

Diversification and Real Estate

Now consider these four levels of diversification in terms of *real estate*. The same sensible rules of basic investment management apply:

1. *Avoid one sector exclusively.* It is not prudent to place all of your real estate–allocated portfolio into speculation in preconstruction condos, or even into single-family fixer-upper houses. Ideally, you want to diversify into different real estate sectors. These may include raw land, mortgages, or multifamily housing.

2. *Be aware that different sectors may be subject to the same cyclical forces.* Even when you own several properties, if they are all subject to the same market forces, all are likely to rise or fall in value for those very reasons. Examples of different sectors that change with identical conditions include single-family

and multifamily rentals, or owning units in different mortgage pools.

3. *Invest in other products as well.* As is true of stocks, it does not make sense to invest all of your money only in real estate, even when you own different types of properties.

4. *Diversify in terms of features of products.* The features of real estate include market risk, liquidity, and a feature not applicable to stocks: *location*. If a specific area is in a price bubble, and it affects all local property, placing all of your capital in the local market exposes all of your capital to the same risks.

DETERMINING YOUR RISK TOLERANCE

As a real estate investor, you need to be aware of three specific forms of risk. For many, the concept of "risk" is limited to the first and best known, which is market risk. But two other risk categories—liquidity risk and leverage risk—are equally important in the overall study of real estate.

Market Risk

Market risk is where the emphasis is placed in any discussion of bubbles. But although price dominates the thinking for most investors and is used as the primary factor in assessing real estate, there is more to market risk. In addition to returning to the fundamentals to *anticipate* changes in real estate trends, investors and speculators may evaluate market risk by observing secondary trends as well. These include changes in local population, job growth or decline, and traffic or commutation patterns. There are many more economic and demographic trends worth watching, but no single one reveals everything; these secondary fundamentals are simply pieces in the larger puzzle that defines market risk and opportunity.

A real estate bubble augments the urgency of market risk based on price. Whenever prices rise or fall, there are specific reasons, and this is a key lesson of market risk. Prices do not change spontaneously in any market or for any product. If you are able to identify the root causes for changes in price—especially when those changes occur rapidly and for no obvious reason—then you are better equipped to anticipate what happens next, to judge levels of risk, and to time decisions with better insight.

Liquidity Risk

The definition of *liquidity risk* has two components. The first component is availability of cash. The concern for cash flow from investment property is a more urgent concern than eventual profits. By definition, real estate is an illiquid asset, and if you own property directly, the only way to get cash out is to refinance. (One exception is the home equity line of credit, or HELOC. Lenders provide homeowners with a line of credit that can be drawn against and repaid conveniently. However, the HELOC is usually not available on rental property, only for owner-occupied houses.)

The second component of the definition of liquidity is your ability to sell. Buying and selling real estate is expensive and time-consuming, but the availability of a "ready market" has to be a concern for everyone. Before committing money to directly owned real estate, it is prudent to set aside a reserve in a more liquid account. Another alternative is to invest in real estate products in which you can invest in relatively small capital increments, and which can be bought and sold on public exchanges. This group includes REITs and real estate ETFs, as discussed in Chapter 8.

Leverage Risk

Leverage risk is the third type of risk to evaluate when balancing real estate against the rest of your portfolio. Most people have seen the ads promoting real estate investment with little or nothing down. You have heard testimonials from people bringing in $10,000 per month without doing any work. The catch, of course, is that you need to sign up for instructions about how to get into the "easy money" real estate. Of course, nothing is really that easy, and buying distressed or foreclosed properties is high risk. Making the kind of profits that these advertisements promise is very difficult and, in most instances, highly unlikely.

You cannot leverage indefinitely in reality, even though it seems to work well on paper. You are told that all you need to do is make a minimum down payment, and then borrow the equity to buy more properties until you own dozens; all will rise in value, and when you sell you double or triple your money. But these wild claims never warn about the risks and the problems you will encounter by speculating in highly leveraged programs. Leverage is a very attractive idea, but the cost of excessive leverage—which includes interest, lender fees and charges, and closing costs on both sides of the transaction—often exceeds the profit you are likely to earn on the properties. Leverage is a tool, but like all tools, it can be abused.

Another point to remember is that distressed properties have been abandoned for a reason. You are not going to find distressed properties with a lot of equity and profit potential. These properties were abandoned specifically because there was little or no equity in the property.

In cases where property values have fallen, marginal buyers can actually save money by walking away from highly leveraged properties. Today, some lenders offer aggressive loan programs, including some that will offer loans *above* current market value. So if a homeowner has borrowed 125 percent of current value and that value later falls, what is the incentive to keep making payments? Prudent lending practices have always been based on the concept that the borrower who has an equity stake in the property will be less likely to abandon it. So when you see distressed or foreclosed properties on the market, chances are good that the property is not a bargain.

BUILDING YOUR PERSONAL FINANCIAL PLAN

Risk analysis is a good first step in building your personal financial plan. This plan should be especially designed by you for your circumstances. Some financial planning offers include written documents called "financial plans." These often consist primarily of boilerplate sections offering standard advice, with little or no tailoring to your specific situation. Rather than taking the time to tell someone else about your income, assets, and investment experience, you can put together a plan for yourself—and save several hundred dollars at the same time.

In developing your own financial plan, it helps to write down its elements. But remember that it is primarily a self-defining document. You will gain insights about how and where to invest by addressing the primary elements, including four major areas:

1. Income and assets
2. Knowledge and experience
3. Anticipated major life events
4. Risk analysis and risk tolerance

Income and Assets

No plan can exceed the limitations of income and assets. So the first important element is identifying exactly what you can afford to invest within your family's budget, and how you will manage and diversify the assets that you set aside for that purpose. Your plan also needs to be set up to adjust when your income and investment asset base grow over time.

Some financial planners like to project ahead and identify the amount you need to save today to reach future goals. Of course, this is highly unreliable because too many variables are involved. These include assumed rates of inflation and future tax rates, the average rate of return you will earn on your investments, and an expected growth in your income. While it is difficult to estimate accurately each of these variables individually, when you add them all together, it is impossible. With this in mind, your financial plan has to be based on what you know today, and must be adjusted periodically as things change in the future.

Knowledge and Experience

Experienced investors know that they need to balance investments with family budget, various kinds of insurance, liquid reserve requirements, and planning for the future. Most "plans" include identification of future goals, such as saving for a child's college education, your retirement, paying off your mortgage, or starting your own business. While goals certainly affect the kinds of investment decisions you make, your knowledge and experience affect the success of your financial plan *and* may also affect the goals you set.

Investment *knowledge* is the range of topics you know well. Many people believe they know about an investment topic, but base their belief on myths or assumptions. So it is important that your knowledge is based on facts rather than on one of the many popular and widespread myths. These myths are not always verbalized, but you can see them in investors' behavior. Although most people know there is no secret formula to beat the market, people still make decisions based on rumor and take more risks than they can afford. The alternative to these errors is to read, study, and observe, and to improve your knowledge base.

Experience is assumed to be the result of gaining and applying knowledge. But so often, experience is what you gain from making mistakes. If you are lucky, your mistakes will not be very expensive ones, and you will be able to use a mix of profits and losses to improve your investment wisdom.

For anyone going into real estate, jumping onto the "bubble bandwagon" may produce profits as long as you devise and employ an exit strategy. Most people do not. As a consequence, losing money in real estate is much easier than people may believe.

Real estate is not a "sure thing," and prices won't rise forever. Everyone realizes this eventually—some from observation and others from bitter and expensive experience.

Anticipated Major Life Events

The major events in life have to be divided into two groups. First are those you control: marriage, having children, buying a home, or changing careers. Second is the group you cannot control: divorce, health problems, uninsured losses, loss of job, and death. But any event in either group must change the entire focus of your financial plan. Because these are *major* events, they directly affect all of your goals, as well as your income and assets. Once you set your financial plan in motion, it has to be reviewed and updated continuously. This review should occur at least once per year and after any major life event.

A common problem among those who have paid for a written financial plan is the assumption that it is permanent. This belief grows from the fact that the document is in writing and was paid for, often involving hundreds of dollars. But if it is true that this document will be obsolete and out of date next year, what value is it? For this reason, it is wiser to think of your financial plan as an evolving thing and not just a document. The plan itself changes just as family budgets change, due to a raise or loss of a job, buying a home, having children, and any number of other changes. A couple married for more than ten years would never consider trying to stick to the budget they used in their first year of marriage. And a budget is a sort of preliminary financial plan aimed at managing and planning for two to four weeks in advance. The same limitations apply to a broader financial plan as well.

Risk Analysis and Risk Tolerance

No one plan is going to work equally well for everyone. In studying a range of possible investments, it is essential that you also analyze the various degrees of risk involved. Most people will agree that the stock market contains higher risks than owning your own home, and that speculating in rapidly growing preconstruction housing has even greater risks. When you consider real estate alternatives (such as mortgage pools, REITs, or real estate ETFs), the various forms of risk are much lower.

Risk analysis is a balancing act, because risk level and potential profit level cannot be separated. The greater the risk, the higher your potential profit or loss will be as well. For this reason, picking an investment appropriate for you involves defining your risk tolerance. How much risk are you willing and able to take? Most people want to diversify their investments in terms of risk. So your real estate investments might include the majority of equity in your own home, some additional funds in lower-risk pooled investments, and perhaps some equity used for speculation.

But however you define your risk tolerance level, you need to understand that profit or loss is a factor of that risk. A real estate ETF is going to yield a return of the *average* components in the portfolio, so that exceptionally high performance will be offset by the exceptionally low components. All pooled funds, due to diversification, are going to yield only the average return. So your money is safer and more available, but the overall return will be lower as well.

COLLECTING YOUR FUNDAMENTALS

Your personal financial planning process begins with the steps outlined in the previous section. You first need to define your level of knowledge and experience, and understand the restrictions of your income and asset base. Then you need to decide how much risk or mix of risks you want to take. Next, you need to pick investments that meet these criteria.

A good starting point is to make a list of investments you believe will be appropriate, and then gather the fundamentals on those investments. This helps you to narrow the list down to the most obvious and appropriate products. For example, the fundamentals within the real estate market will help you to identify whether a bubble exists in your city. When the inventory of properties is excessive and it takes a long time for properties to sell, these are signs of oversupply. When this happens while property values continue to rise, it is the classic bubble. The point here is that you can discover the bubble by examining the fundamentals.

The fundamentals define the markets. This is true in all three submarkets (supply and demand for property, the rental market, and the financing market), and knowing the fundamentals affecting each makes you an effective analyst of the market.

More commonly, investors tend to react only to growing prices of properties, and often decide to "get into the market" primarily because prices are rising so fast. This is the classic *modus operandi* in the market: buy high and sell low. The same people who get into the market because prices are rising (or more to the point, have *already* risen) are also likely to panic and sell once the bubble bursts.

Using the Information

How do you react to the fundamentals once you have identified current market conditions? Ideally, the fundamentals within a normal (non-bubble) cycle will help you to identify the cyclical points at which buying real estate makes sense. This basic idea of buying real estate as an investment when prices are fair, inventory of homes is limited, and homes are selling within a few weeks and close to asked price, should be your goal as an investor. Speculators do not usually look at any of these factors, and they stand to earn larger short-term profits *and* to suffer much larger short-term losses.

An analysis of the fundamentals also points out when timing is poor. This analysis can be valuable even if it only tells you to stay out of the market until conditions change. When property

values are inflated, you can stay out of the market, sell investments you currently own, or sell options.

When prices are low, you can use the fundamentals to time
an entry into the market as well. This may involve buying property in the traditional manner at depressed prices (and ignoring
the pervasive mood of fear in the market), or buying up options
to fix prices over a period of time (three years is common for
leases and usually for lease-option contracts as well). In either
event, you can hold properties as a landlord and cover your costs
through rents (assuming the rental market fundamentals support
this plan, of course).

In the case of the traditional buy-and-hold strategy, rents
have to be high enough to cover your mortgage and other payments, *and* you need to be willing to accept the risks of potential
vacancies and unexpected expenses and repairs. In the case of a
lease-option, you actually have far less risk. The rent you receive
should be high enough to cover the lease payment you are required to make. In the ideal situation, it may also cover your option cost. At the end of the lease term, you can simply walk away
from the deal if values have not risen. And at any time during the
option term, you can exercise and earn a profit. So the plan provides you with a lot of flexibility.

Tracking Trend Changes

Any investor can use fundamental analysis to study the market
beyond the obvious. In real estate, the obvious refers to market
value. The vast majority of stories you hear about real estate involve the rapid and high profits other people have earned in
property speculation or investment. You rarely hear about losses
or even flat markets when other people tell you their stories. But
even though obsession with price dominates investor thinking in
real estate, you can use fundamental analysis to gain more powerful insights.

In real estate (and in other markets as well) the most valuable information anticipates what is going to happen next. Most people react to what happened before, so that opportunities may have already been lost. This is why most people buy high and sell low. Fundamentals do not only identify the current condition of the market; they can also be used to identify when trends are about to change.

Trends are subtle. But when you combine fundamentals to track a trend, you begin to get a keen sense of the cyclical strength in movements, changes in the trend itself, and pending reversals. This is possible because you combine information on two levels:

1. *A Study of All the Fundamentals Working Together.* You cannot look at a single factor and determine with any accuracy the current state of the market. You need to review all of the fundamentals. The concept of *confirmation* is essential, because trends invariably give many false starts. Short-term markets are chaotic, and the only way to know when a shift in a trend is significant is when two or more of the fundamentals reveal the same thing.

2. *Analysis of the Fundamentals in All Three Real Estate Submarkets.* The fundamentals of the three submarkets—supply and demand, rentals, and financing—can and do work in tandem in some regions, and can be used to confirm each other. However, in other regions these submarkets may work in opposition to one another or in complete disregard for changes in the market. For example, in a city whose population consists primarily of a retirement population of homeowners *and* a large college-aged renter group, you cannot expect the supply-and-demand market to track the rental market or to confirm trends. The two are distinct and separate because the demographics of the market are dissimilar. They coexist in the same region, but there is no crossover between the two markets.

BECOME YOUR OWN EXPERT

As long as you study the fundamentals of real estate and understand the distinctions of the submarkets, you will be far ahead of
most investors and speculators. By concentrating on the fundamentals, you will become an expert in local real estate.

The widespread belief that real estate professionals are experts is false. Most insiders include real estate salespeople, local
lenders, and financial planners. There are important reasons why
none of these real estate "experts" can fully comprehend what
drives the market

Real Estate Salespeople

First of all, salespeople are compensated by way of commissions.
So if would-be sellers ask, "Is this a good time to list my home?"
they will invariably be given a list of reasons why listing is
smarter today than ever before. If would-be buyers ask, "Is this
a good time to buy a home?" the same result has to be expected.
For those compensated on a commission basis, there is never a
bad time to buy or to sell. But the reason these insiders don't
understand the market goes even deeper.

Real estate salespeople may be extremely professional and
know how to maximize a home's market appeal, how to find good
values, and how to write listings. But many do not understand
the real estate market or its cycles, the cause and effect of bubbles, or the placement of real estate in various forms or within a
larger portfolio. If a local agent is going to be paid when a home
sells, can you expect the same agent to advise you to put some
capital into a REIT or ETF? The core emphasis of a real estate
salesperson is going to be generating listings and sales. Even the
most experienced and highly trained agents and brokers are
going to share this limitation. There is a conflict of interest.

Local Lenders

Because they do not put money at risk in the same manner as
investors do, local lenders do not know how to assess risks. They

only know how to comply with the requirements of the secondary market. So even when a local lender services a loan, the actual loan *risk* usually goes into one of the big mortgage pools or, at the very least, is guaranteed by one of the quasi-government agencies providing secondary market services. As discussed before, since 1970 lenders no longer need cash reserves, which used to limit their loan portfolio. Because the entire lending industry has been relegated to the role of secondary market agent, you cannot expect lenders to know how to judge local values. Think of the lender as a source of capital, but not as the actual provider of that capital.

Lenders focus on whether borrowers meet the requirements, and on how much appraisers will state that properties are worth. They rarely need to ask, "Is this property a good risk for the lender?" or "Is this borrower a good risk for repayment of the loan?" They only need to match up a borrower's income to the percentage requirements of the secondary market, and process loans to generate the fees paid to them for their service.

Financial Planners

Planners have the same vested interest as real estate salespeople—they make money from commissions. Even fee-based planners have an incentive to direct clients to load mutual funds, because these funds pay a sales commission to the financial planner. It is rare to find a financial planner who understands investment real estate or the cyclical nature of the real estate market. Their emphasis tends to be on stock-based and bond-based investments, track record, and returns. In fact, the capital you invest in real estate is likely to be viewed by financial planners as capital not available to invest in products that generate a commission.

For these reasons, financial planners—though they may be viewed as being experts in all types of investments—usually have a very narrow focus for their clientele. This means that you have to become your own expert if you want to be able to make objective decisions about how and when to invest.

A BROAD VIEW OF BUBBLES

If you are going to buy and sell investment property, you need to be able to accept some losses. Just as stock market investors sometimes win and sometimes lose, real estate investors and speculators cannot expect 100 percent success. Even so, many people do expect 100 percent when they enter the real estate market.

The myth that real estate is a "sure thing" has misled many people and has allowed investors to take on a false sense of security. This is especially true in the ill-advised certainty seen at the height of a bubble-based frenzy.

When real estate prices rise year after year, it is natural for developers to build more and more. The demand is there, so why would a developer ignore it, especially if the property is sold in advance? The virtually unlimited financing offered by lenders only makes the situation worse, and facilitates a bigger bubble, meaning bigger losses when it does pop.

You can and should resist temptation to jump into real estate because prices are rising, without first checking the fundamentals. Rising prices are not always caused by bubbles, and there might be sound reasons to buy today. But without checking the fundamentals, you cannot know for certain. Avoid what so many speculators have fallen for: the belief that you will somehow know exactly when to get out of the market. So many people who have lost money thought they would get out just before prices began to fall and, of course, they were wrong.

Remember the bubble rule: *The more money you make, the more you want to reinvest; and the more you reinvest, the more you will lose.* This is the invariable tendency for speculators in real estate and in all other markets. It is the "greed factor" at work and, like the "fear factor," it is difficult to resist.

Contrary to the belief that by being in the market you will somehow know exactly when to get out, it is more likely that you will not recognize the signs of change. There may be any number of regional bubbles in existence at any one time. But the extreme points of view have to be taken with suspicion.

First is the view that there really are no bubbles and only the overly conservative investor buys into the theory of the bubble. These believers cite the efficient market hypothesis to "prove" that, logically, there cannot be any such thing as a bubble. But the hypothesis is just that, and it is often provably wrong.

The second point of view tells you that *all* real estate is going to crash at the same time. So you should get out now, sell your house and all real estate holdings, and wait out the coming real estate recession. But because all markets are regional, this belief is based on hysteria and fear and should be discounted.

In a larger investment perspective, real estate should play a key role in your portfolio. For many decades, well-researched investment in single-family housing has proven to be a sound move, not only financially but also because it provides a family with security and growing equity. Home ownership represents a majority of financial equity for most people, and this trend is likely to continue indefinitely.

For any investment beyond purchase of your own home, you have a range of choices, from the very conservative pooled investment market all the way through to the highly speculative.

You can better succeed in real estate by first defining your own risk tolerance, and then matching your investments to meet that definition. In any market—and real estate is no exception—the research you do in advance of committing funds pays off because *informed* decisions are invariably *smart* decisions. Real estate involves more than the price and price trend; it is ingrained in the American culture. In fact, one author, discussing this cultural aspect of real estate, observed that:

One thing Americans demonstrably have done better than any other culture in history—for centuries—is handle chaos and change, and invent the future. Americans are part of a wildly individualistic, determined culture that may or may not know how to resolve dilemmas, but that does attack obstacles— compulsively and reflexively. Americans believe, endearingly and in spite of all evidence, that for every problem, there is a solution.[1]

This applies to predictable, safe economic times as well as to bubbles. No matter what circumstances, chaos and change are constants; and the American real estate investor survives, adjusts, and overcomes whatever obstacles the market devises.

NOTE

1. Joel Garreau, *Edge City* (New York: Anchor Books, 1992), Introduction.

Bibliography

Benke, William and Joseph Fowler. *All About Real Estate Investing.* McGraw-Hill, 2001.

Berges, Steve. *The Complete Guide to Real Estate Finance for Investment Properties.* John Wiley and Sons, 2004.

Bonner, William. *Financial Reckoning Day.* John Wiley and Sons, 2003.

Bronchick, William, and Robert Dahlstrom. *Flipping Properties.* Dearborn, 2001.

Duncan, Richard. *The Dollar Crisis.* John Wiley and Sons, 2003.

Faber, Marc. *Tomorrow's Gold.* CLSA Books, 2003.

Fridsonh, Martin. *It Was a Very Good Year.* John Wiley and Sons, 1998.

Gallinelli, Frank. *What Every Real Estate Investor Needs to Know About Cash Flow.* McGraw-Hill, 2004.

Garreau, Joel. *Edge City.* Anchor Books, 1992.

Goodman, Jordan. *Everyone's Money Book on Real Estate.* Dearborn, 2002.

Mackay, Charles. *Extraordinary Popular Delusions and the Madness of Crowds.* Richard Bentley, 1841.

McLean, Andrew, and Gary Eddred. *Investing in Real Estate, 4th Edition.* John Wiley and Sons, 2003.

Myers, Kevin. *But It, Fix It, Sell It, Profit!* Dearborn, 1998.

Pivar, William. *Real Estate Investing from A to Z, 3rd Edition.* McGraw-Hill, 2004.

Rubino, John. *How to Profit from the Coming Real Estate Bust.* Rodale, 2003.

Shemin, Robert. *Successful Real Estate Investing.* John Wiley and Sons, 2005.

Talbott, John. *The Coming Crash in the Housing Market.* Mc-Graw-Hill, 2003.

Willis, Gerri. *The Smart Money Guide to Real Estate Investing.* John Wiley and Sons, 2003.

Resources

The following sites provide links to other sites, free and subscription-based statistics, and other valuable information for real estate investors:

American Bankers Association
www.aba.com

American Planning Association
www.planning.org

American Real Estate Society
www.aresnet.org

American Real Estate and Urban Economics Association
www.areuea.org

apartments.com
www.apts.com

Appraisal Foundation
www.appraisalfoundation.org

Appraisal Institute
www.appraisalinstitute.org

Axiometrics Inc.
www.axiometrics.com

Bankrate.com
www.bankrate.com

Best Places to Live
www.bestplaces.net

Bizloan
www.bizloan.org

Building Owners and Managers Association
www.boma.org

Bureau of Economic Analysis
www.bea.doc.gov

Bureau of Labor Statistics
www.bls.gov

CACI, International
www.caci.com

Census Bureau
www.census.gov

Century 21
www.century21.com/learn/glossary.aspx

City Design Center
www.uic.edu/aa/cdc

Claritas.com
www.claritas.com

Congress for the New Urbanism
www.cnu.org

Demographics USA
www.tradedimensions.com

Dividend Discount Model
www.dividenddiscountmodel.com

Economic Development Administration
www.eda.gov

Economy.com
www.economy.com

Fed World
www.fedworld.gov

Federal Home Loan Mortgage Corporation
www.freddiemac.com

Federal Housing Administration
www.fha-home-loans.com

Federal National Mortgage Association
www.fanniemae.com/index.jhtml

Federal Reserve Financial Services
www.frbservices.org

GlobeSt.com
www.globest.com

Government National Mortgage Association
www.ginniemae.gov

Homeglossary.com
www.homeglossary.com

HomeSearcher.com
www.homeresearcher.com

Hoovers Online
www.hoovers.com/free

Housing and Urban Development
www.hud.gov

Housing Zone
www.housingzone.com

HSH Associates Financial Publishers
www.hsh.com/calc-amort.html

Institute of Real Estate Management
www.irem.org

Institutional Real Estate
www.irei.com

Interest.com
mortgages.interest.com

InterestRateCalculators.com
www.interestratecalculator.com

International Economic Development Council
www.iedconline.org

Joint Center for Housing Studies
www.jchs.harvard.edu

Law.com
www.dictionary.law.com

Mortgage Bankers Association of America
www.mbaa.org

Mortgage Guaranty Insurance Corporation
www.mgic.com

Mortgage-loan-search.com
www.mortgage-loan-search.com

MSN house and home
houseandhome.msn.com

Multiple Listing Service
www.mls.org

National Association of Homebuilders
www.nahb.org

National Association of Mortgage Bankers
www.namb.org

National Association of Real Estate Investment Managers
www.nareim.org

National Association of Real Estate Investment Trusts
www.nareit.org

National Association of Realtors
www.realtor.org

National Association of Residential Property Managers
www.narpm.org

National Multi Housing Council
www.nmhc.org

National Real Estate Investor
www.nreionline.com

NPA Data
www.economy.com/default.asp

Office of Federal Housing Enterprise Oversight
www.ofheo.gov

Owners.com
www.owners.com

Real Estate Investment Advisory Council
www.reiac.org

Real Estate Research Institute
www.reri.org

Real-estate-law.freeadvice
real-estate-law.freeadvice.com

Reals.com
www.reals.com

REITnetOnline
www.reitnet.com

State Tax Central
www.statetaxcentral.com

Urban Land Institute
www.uli.org

Veterans Affairs
www.va.gov

World Factbook
www.odci.gov/cia/publications/factbook

Yahoo! real estate
realestate.yahoo.com/re/homevalues

Index

Look for These Exciting Real Estate Titles at www.amacombooks.org/realestate

A Survival Guide for Buying a Home by Sid Davis $17.95

A Survival Guide for Selling a Home by Sid Davis $15.00

Are You Dumb Enough to Be Rich? by G. William Barnett II $18.95

Everything You Need to Know Before Buying a Co-op, Condo, or Townhouse by Ken Roth $18.95

Home Makeovers That Sell by Sid Davis $15.00

Make Millions Selling Real Estate by Jim Remley $18.95

Mortgages 101 by David Reed $16.95

Mortgage Confidential by David Reed $16.95

Real Estate Investing Made Simple by M. Anthony Carr $17.95

Real Estate Presentations That Make Millions by Jim Remley $18.95

The Complete Guide to Investing in Foreclosures by Steve Berges $17.95

The Consultative Real Estate Agent by Kelle Sparta $17.95

The Home Buyer's Question and Answer Book by Bridget McCrea $16.95

The Landlord's Financial Tool Kit by Michael C. Thomsett $18.95

The Property Management Tool Kit by Mike Beirne $19.95

The Real Estate Agent's Business Planner by Bridget McCrea $19.95

The Real Estate Agent's Field Guide by Bridget McCrea $19.95

The Real Estate Investor's Pocket Calculator by Michael C. Thomsett $17.95

The Successful Landlord by Ken Roth $19.95

Who Says You Can't Buy a Home! by David Reed $17.95

Your Successful Real Estate Career, Fifth Edition, by Kenneth W. Edwards $18.95

Available at your local bookstore, online, or call 800-250-5308

Savings start at 35% on Bulk Orders of 5 copies or more!

Save up to 55%!

For details, contact AMACOM Special Sales
Phone: 212-903-8316. E-mail: SpecialSls@amanet.org